Infusion

From Apartness to Non-Duality

Nigel Wentworth

There is no copyright on the words or ideas in this book.

ISBN: 978-0-244-09612-0

To Andrea

Contents

Introduction

Nothing written here is true. It might seem so by the conventional standards of society accepted by human beings, but one of the questions asked here concerns the validity of these conventions; and what will be suggested is that they are wanting.

What is being talked about is a mystery, a mystery that cannot be understood and so cannot be put into words. Whatever can be said is only an inadequate proxy for it. Words are only pointers that gesture towards that which is, which remains ultimately indescribable.

What is being talked about here is intrinsically experiential and so the only way to gauge it is to see if it coincides with lived-experience. Being experiential it is also perspectival and does not recognise anything that is not. All utterances are perspectival; an expression of the perspective from which they are made. It is one of the delusions of reason and thought that it believes that it is possible to arrive at a truth that is beyond, or outside of, any perspective.

What follows is not a theology or philosophy that pretends to be true, to be the way reality actually is. Rather it is a series of stories and descriptions with conclusions and generalisations drawn out from them that may or may not be found to be helpful. One of the conclusions is that any pretence that a story, description or generalisation could be the truth about the way reality actually is, is vain.

The Story

When I was young I always knew that there was something more to everything than the way other people spoke about and related to it all. For most people, a tree seemed to be just a 'tree' and a chair just a 'chair'; both mere things. They seemed to experience every thing as if it was a mere functional object. It seemed to me that in this way of relating to things something important had been lost. This was, for me, particularly true in relation to the visual world. There was something wondrous and infinite about the visual world that no amount of words could ever capture and which seemed to be denied by the way that other people appeared to relate to it and talk about it. In that way of talking and relating it was as if everything had been reduced to an empty shell of itself, as if everything that really mattered had been lost.

But for some reason, that I could not understand, no one else seemed to have a problem with this. Everyone appeared to get on as if it was all quite straightforward and nothing was amiss. So, on some level, I formed an assumption that it was not they but rather I who was missing something and that somehow everything could not really be as it seemed to me that it was. I was mistaken and needed to learn to take the world at face value the way that others seemed to. That struggle, to belong to and get by in the world that others appeared to find quite straightforward, formed the background to the circumstantial details of my life for many years. But it always felt as if something, somehow the most important thing, was missing, or had been lost; though I could also never imagine how it could possibly return. Then, one day, that invisible door was found and passed through which brought me back to the world part of me had always inhabited and which I now realised had always been there. And the struggle stopped.

Chapter One

Sitting on the Floor in Paris

Up to the age of fifteen I got along in the manner of a typically dysfunctional teenager but then, in matter of a few weeks, something fundamental shifted and the bottom fell out of my life. The core of this shift seemed towards a much deeper self-awareness. I became aware of myself as what I called an 'atomistic individual', that is a person completely apart from everybody else. The sense I had was that I was free to do what I wanted, had complete autonomy and could lead my life as I chose, subject to the usual constraints of money and practical necessity. In principle, however, aside from these constraints I was an autonomous being, apart from everybody else, with the freedom to live out my life, until my death, however I wanted. Experiencing myself and my life in this way brought on a chronic sense of aloneness and isolation. I felt, in a deep way, apart from everybody and everything and therefore utterly alone.

At the same time, and probably as simply another manifestation of the same shift, I felt cut off and cast out. It was as if I had lost something immeasurably precious. Something in me was aware that it had not always been like this. At some point in the past this sense of aloneness and loss had not been there and things had felt very different. But that had somehow been lost and now I felt utterly bereft. I did not know what had been lost, there was just a sense that something had been, something immeasurably precious, and that before that at some point much earlier in life it had not been like this. It made me think of the story of Adam and Eve being cast out of the Garden of Eden. How I felt was how I imagined they would have felt; though at the time I did not think more deeply about the meaning of the story and its deeper connection with what was going on for me.

Alongside feeling like an atomistic individual, cast out and alone, I also came to be aware that everything that I did I did for myself. If I went out with friends, it was because I thought that it would be enjoyable for me. If I worked at my studies it was so as to gain good qualifications for myself, and I wanted these so that one day I could get a good job, again for myself. And I wanted that so that I would earn money, so that I could one day buy a house, have a car, go on holidays and do the things that I wanted to do. All of it was me doing things for myself.

It also seemed clear to me that this was what everybody else was doing too; everybody, not just the people around me, but the whole of humanity. Everything that I did and everybody else as well was simply 'the self trying to get something for itself' as I described it to myself. Even things that did not on the surface appear to be self-driven it seemed clear to me were in fact just that. So people being 'altruistic' and doing things for others rather than themselves was really something that they only did because ultimately they thought they would feel better that way. They had realised that doing things directly for themselves was not very fulfilling and that doing things for others made them feel better. So they did that. But really, it was still the self trying to get something for itself. It seemed clear that there was nothing that people ever did that was not that.

This activity of the self, always trying to get something for itself, seemed like a kind of constant struggle to try to make one's experience as good as possible. Negative experiences were avoided and positive ones sought. It was as if everyone had a kind of internal balance sheet of experience that they were continually trying to shore up, so as to keep it in the black and stop it from falling into deficit.

This whole process seemed completely empty and vain to me and yet I became aware over time that I could not just stop it. When I was by myself I noticed that I did not feel at all good. There was always a sense of lack, of something being missing, like a kind of inner emptiness or sadness. I found it uncomfortable and did not like it. To get away from it I would come up with some idea or another of something that I could do, which I believed would make me feel better. And I would then go and do it. If it worked I would feel better; for a bit. But inevitably the sense of inner emptiness, or lack, that uncomfortable feeling of something being missing or having been lost, would come back again. And then the whole cycle would start up again and I would find myself thinking of something else that I could do to try to make myself feel better.

It was clear that the problem was a lot deeper than the ways in which I tried to deal with it. It was not simply a matter of feeling a bit bored and so watching television or going out to see friends. That sort of thing did not begin to solve the problem and it always came back exactly the same as before once I stopped watching television or left my friends. Nor was it simply about not being good enough at something, for however well I did at anything it still came back. Yes, there were short periods of satisfaction, such as when I was amusing myself with friends, or when I had done well at something at school; but it never lasted very long and the gnawing sense of inner lack and dissatisfaction would always come back again, often very quickly. It felt like endlessly trying to shore up a dam so as to hold back the floodwaters that were threatening to overwhelm it. The whole of life seemed to be made up of what I later came to hear described as 'cycles of becoming'. Some were very short, lasting only a short while, like reading a book, others stretched into the distance and went on for years, like getting qualifications. With the latter, what was done today was just a small contribution to an enormous cycle of becoming, at the end of which was promised a major sense of achievement and fulfilment. At root, however, it seemed very clear to me that it was all really the same thing. It was all the self trying to get something for itself, so as to make itself feel better. And the reason it was doing that was because it did not feel good enough as it was.

What also became clear was that nothing was ever really 'better'. Yes, things could be made different. I could one day end up with qualifications, even good ones, or I could end up with no qualifications. I could have and see more friends, or I could end up more and more on my own. That was true, but nothing to do with anything like this changed the underlying situation. Whatever happened, I was still there, feeling cut off, cast out and with a chronic sense of inner lack that did not go away.

What came out of this was a complete loss of faith in the possibility of anything really making a difference. I stopped believing that it was possible for a person's life really to get better. With that I also lost faith that it was really possible to make anything better in a wider sense, in society, the world, anything. The belief people seemed to have that it was possible to make the world a better place seemed like a grotesque delusion. Looking around me it seemed obvious that though certain things had got better during the twentieth century, for instance medicine, other things had also got worse, for instance, we now had nuclear bombs and environmental threats to the planet. Also, I simply did not believe that people were really happier now than they used to be. Life might be quite different in certain superficial ways, but ultimately on a deeper level it seemed to me that it was really just the same thing and so people's levels of happiness would be basically the same.

If anything, I formed a belief that ultimately things were getting worse. I used to read a lot of history and formed a romanticised picture of the past before the industrial revolution as a time when life was simpler, lived closer to the soil and with less of the constant noise, distraction and artificiality of modern life. And I believed that I would have been happier in a time like that. In short, I wanted to run away.

Part of what I was aware that I was running away from was death. During the few weeks when something profound shifted in my awareness, as well as coming to see myself as an atomistic individual, cut off and cast out, I also became aware of death as a kind of living reality. It felt as if one day death had walked into my life, not as some kind of distant eventuality but instead as a living presence. There was an almost physical sense of death, as a kind of being in my life. It followed me around and seemed to hover above me looking over my shoulder. Everything that happened seemed to do so in the context of death. So, if I was at school, or doing some work, or with friends or thinking of doing something to distract myself, death would be there too. Everything that happened would be played out in front of it and measured up against it. The question I constantly found myself asking was this, 'given that death is real what is the point of 'this?", about whatever it was that I was doing. And in that context everything was found wanting. Given the reality of death nothing appeared to have any meaning at all. With everything being experienced in this way, whatever I did felt utterly meaningless. And this feeling, the feeling of the meaninglessness of everything, became the abiding experience of my life.

This feeling of meaninglessness was grounded upon all of these things that I had become aware of at this time. I could not see the point of doing anything to try to make things better for myself, whether it be reading a book, playing sport or working at my studies, or anything really, when I always came back to the same experience of inner loss and dissatisfaction afterwards. I could not see the point of trying to find a place of temporary belonging in the world, when I felt consumed by a sense of having been cast out. There seemed to be no point in seeing people, when I felt inwardly chronically alone. And it seemed utterly meaningless trying to accumulate positive experiences for myself when one day – a day that seemed very real – I was going to die and it would all come to nought? The whole of life felt utterly pointless and my capacity to carry on, in the way that everybody else seemed able to do, just collapsed.

For years, this sense of meaninglessness racked my whole body. It was a palpable physical sensation, not just an abstract idea. Almost everything seemed imbued with a sense of utter pointlessness that made carrying on impossible. The only respite came when I was absorbed in some activity or another, the work which I did for my living – repairing photocopying machines – seemed to work best in this respect. Then the sense of meaninglessness would be temporarily absent; though as soon as I came back to myself, as I put it as soon as I was 'present to myself' again, or self-conscious, it would be there. At best, this feeling of the meaninglessness of everything became the low-level background against which everything happened, at worst it brought on a chronic feeling of anguish that would annihilate any capacity to function that I had. Quite rapidly, my whole life fell apart. I lost touch with the friends I had had, became very isolated and could no longer function 'normally' by society's standards. Eventually, I dropped out of school, then university and finally art school in Paris.

Being a person at all seemed to me quite unbearable. The continual cycles of becoming that seemed to make up my life seemed utterly pointless and all I wanted was for it all to stop. And yet it would not. I seemed condemned to an existence on a hamster wheel of endlessly feeling a sense of lack, doing something to try to get to a better place, achieving a short term feeling of satisfaction, before coming back to my original place of lack again. I used to look at trees and yearned to be able to be like them; simply able to 'be' – as I understood it – without any striving to get anywhere. But nothing was more impossible for me. I felt consumed by a vast, churning, driving energy, full of dissatisfaction, giving way to a constant movement onto the next thing. I was completely unable to 'be', to be still and quiet or at peace. If I tried to be like this, it was clear that it was just another thing that I was doing because I believed that I would be better off like that. It was clear that it was still the self trying to get something for itself and so was full of the same self-seeking as everything else. I could see all this, see myself trying to get to a better place by trying to be still. The contradiction was palpable, the contradiction of someone trying to *be*, trying to be still, in order to try to get to a better place for themselves. It was pure becoming, the very opposite of 'being'.

I became quite depressed and over the next lot of years often thought about ending my life. What always stopped me was part of what brought me there in the first place, the sense of having lost something and being consequently cast out. Somewhere inside me was a sense of this thing I had lost. I did not know what it was, but the sense of it was palpable, especially in my darkest moments of despair. And with that came a sense that I could find it again. That was always how I turned the corner, on the descent into oblivion, and came back to life again. Over time it became a kind of conviction, something that I held to deep within myself, sharing it with no one, but which ultimately kept me going.

It was always clear to me that everyone experiences something of this inner dissatisfaction, though for most it is clearly not as acute and so the manifestation not so dramatic. But the evidence that everybody, ultimately, has a similar experience of life is everywhere; for no one is able just to *be*. The human condition is one of continual becoming. People are always on a movement *to* somewhere, towards something, trying to get something for themselves which they believe will somehow make their experience better. The cycles of becoming are complex and varied, but it is always the same basic pattern. People do not feel alright, whole or complete just as they are. Somewhere, however subtly or unconsciously, there is a sense of something being amiss, or of something lacking. Out of this grows up a sense of dissatisfaction. And then thought steps in with a suggestion of something that it proposes might alleviate the sense of lack and the person will follow this, trying to get this thing, trying to get to this place. If it succeeds a temporary sense of fulfilment arises, of wholeness and completion and of nothing being lacking, but it is always temporary and the deeper sense of lack always returns.

Many years later, I heard this process described as 'seeking'. Everybody is a seeker; because everybody experiences the same sense of inner lack and everybody tries to assuage it by a movement to find that which will make them feel whole again. And for most people their whole lives are played out in this way. What they typically seek are the usual things, a good job, enough money to be comfortable, a nice home, a partner for life and enough pleasures and treats to keep themselves going. It is never experienced as being entirely satisfactory though – for if it was it would stop – but it seems to work well enough to feel just about good enough. And so it carries on.

This path did not seem open to me. Just thinking about it seemed unbearable; I imagine because it seemed like accepting living with the sense of anguish and meaninglessness forever and I knew I could not do that. I had to find another way. I could not just 'be' because of all the churning desires and impulses that arose within me. Nor did it make any difference which kinds of desires I pursued; it all felt equally meaningless. So, I came to believe that it was the very existence of the desires that was the problem. This led me to form the idea, like so many before me, of trying to be free of these desires by denying them and not giving in to them. In short, I became an ascetic. For ten years I pursued a regime of fasting, sleeping on the floor, having cold showers, eating and dressing inadequately and in general denying the impulses that arose within me, particularly if giving in to them would have made life more pleasant and comfortable. The end result, to cut a very long story short, was that it did not work. The desires, I learnt, could not be quelled in this way. The more I resisted them, in fact, the stronger they seemed to get. Not eating only made me think constantly about food, sleeping on the floor only made me sleep badly and so crave and think about sleep even more and so on. I kept going for so long only because the alternative, just giving into my desires and ending up with what society seemed to consider a 'normal' life felt so unbearable. Eventually, worn down by the deprivation and strain, my health gave way and I had to stop.

During this time, alongside the sense of the meaninglessness of worldly self-seeking, I also had a sense that I had lost touch with who I really was. I had no idea who I really was but knew that it was not who and what I had become. I sensed that my upbringing in my family, my schooling with its endless pressure for academic success and society with its pressure to be like everybody else had made me into a person that was not my real self. This consciousness formed itself around the same time as I became aware of death and started to feel cast out and cut off from everything. At the time I did not really understand it. Now it all seems quite clear: through the conditioning that a human being is subject to during their lives, particularly in the formative years at the beginning, a 'person' comes into being, with a particular identity. This identity is something that the person carries with them and which they see themselves as being. It might be being white, working class, female, musical and sensitive, amongst many other things, or it could be being Asian, Muslim, male, devout, hard-working and serious. It does not matter. Whatever it is, it is an assumed, or constructed, identity. Out of this constructed identity arise the roles that the person has in his or her life and the fulfilment of which makes up so much of the process of living.

At the time, as I have said, I did not understand all this. All I knew was that I did not feel like the 'person' that I had become. My identity was that of a Westerner living in a highly industrialised society, I was middle class and bright with all the typical expectations that went with that and I was the second son in a highly political family of six. And I did not really feel any of it. There seemed to be a gap of some sort between that, the identity I had with all the elements that made it up, and the roles that went with them, and who I really was, or how I felt myself really to be. I did not know what this latter was and could not say anything at all about it. All I knew was that it was not the same thing as this identity that I seemed to have become. This sense that I was not really my identity never left me in later life, no matter how much I seemed to 'fill out' as an adult. There was always a sense that something was awry and did not fit. The way other people were and the way the world appeared to function, seemed like a game of charades in which everybody was playing an assumed role. Somehow, it never felt real. When this first arose around the age of sixteen, because I believed that it was my involvement with other people and in society in general that had led me to lose touch with myself as I had, my answer to this was to decide that I needed to isolate myself from everyone and everything in order to find myself again. This was again something that I did for most of ten years and contributed to the general sense of strain that ultimately led to its collapse. Even after it collapsed, however, the sense that I was not really my social identity never left me and for thirty five years I was a seeker after who I really was.

Most people who reject mainstream seeking – money, career, home, pleasure – become religious seekers, for instance Christians or Buddhists or modern spiritual seekers, joining a sect or following a particular guru or teacher. I looked at these things, but what I saw did not look very different from the mainstream seeking of 'normal' life. Goals were dangled like carrots in front of seekers, for instance that they might get to heaven, or become enlightened, on condition that they did certain things. It was true that the goals were very different from the goals of conventional seeking, but overall the structures seemed exactly the same. It was still something that someone would do in order to get something for themselves. Whether someone is told that they can get rich if only they will work hard and save, or that they can be happy if they sort themselves out through therapy, or if they are told that they can become enlightened if they meditate and follow the four-fold path, or if they are told that they can become more fulfilled and at peace if they learn to live in the moment, did not seem very different to me. To follow any of these paths was still to be a self trying to get something for itself, and I was aware that this was certainly my motivation in thinking about moving in this direction. As soon as I saw that the old feeling of the utter meaninglessness of self-seeking returned and with it the impossibility of carrying on down any path like this.

As well as experiencing religious and spiritual practices as just another form of self-seeking, their injunctions that one should pray or meditate or try to live in the moment seemed to go against what for me was my most basic motivation in the first place. Feeling anguished by my sense of self-hood, with the constant drive to self-seek that seemed to come with it, all I wanted was to be able to 'be', like a tree or a bird. But trees, or birds, or clouds, or stones, did not need to *do* anything in order to be. They just were that anyway. Everything else was that, without having to try to be it, except people. We seemed to be the only things in the world that were unable to be and instead lived an existence of constant becoming. And now, because we were unable to just be, we were being told to do all sorts of things in order to learn to be able to be again. But to me it just did not make sense. I could not see how being, which was the opposite of becoming, could be learnt through a process of becoming. I simply could never believe that I could ever come to be, like a tree, by trying to do something or trying to get somewhere. It just seemed obvious. Nothing else needed to do this, so why did we? It seemed like a wrong turn to me, and I could not follow it. Rather than me needing to learn to do something new now, in order to get back to being able to just be, I felt that what needed to happen was for something that had already happened to be undone as it were. Something must have happened to make me unable to be. It had been how I was once, I felt sure, because I was aware that before the change that took place around my sixteenth birthday I had not felt anguished and constantly driven to self-seek. Also, the sense of having lost something or been cast out from something was palpable. What I believed needed to happen was the undoing of whatever it was that had happened which had taken me away from being able to 'be' and then what had been lost would naturally be found again. I had no idea how this could happen. All I was clear about was that pursuing a path of becoming could not be the answer.

For these reasons, I was never a conventional spiritual seeker, belonging to a religion or following a guru. Instead, my path was the rather stony one of asceticism and isolation, of trying to resist the desires and impulses that I felt. The only desire that for years I made no attempt to resist was the one to escape from the feeling of anguish that beset me whenever I was 'present to myself'. I found this anguish so unbearable that doing anything other than trying to get away from it seemed impossible. Whenever it arose, it would quite rapidly get stronger and stronger until my whole body was racked with it. It was an awful feeling and one that I found unbearable. So, whenever it arose I would try and get away from it, generally by distracting myself in one way or another.

This carried on for eight years until I was twenty three. I have no idea why, but at that point one day I simply could not carry on living the way I had been for so many years, feeling a kind of constant anguish and endlessly trying to escape from it into a temporary distraction, like working or going for a walk. I eventually reached a point of utter desperation and despair. For some reason, I arrived at a place where I could no longer bear the endless cycle of feeling the anguish rise up in me and then running away from it. I had got to a place where I really felt that it would be better to die rather than to carry on living like that. I felt that whatever came of facing the anguish rather than running away from it would be better than what I had been doing for so long. So, the next day when it arose again, instead of running away I just sat down on the floor and did not try to get away from it. The feeling of anguish got stronger and stronger, as it always did, and after a very short time I could bear it no more. I got up, went out of my flat in Paris, down the six flights of stairs and out into the street to get away. The same thing happened the next day and the day after that for a number of days. Until one day, when I was sitting there, and the thought came up to get out and get away from this unbearable feeling, another thought came in asking why I wanted to go. There was a reply to that question, something like 'to get away from this feeling', but then another question arose about that, leading to another answer and so on. I do not know how many questions and answers there were, but a number, until eventually there was a question to which no answer arose. Then, suddenly, I was not there any more and nor was the room I was sitting in or anything at all. All there was, was something like light, or presence. When I thought about it afterwards I had no idea what had happened, or what it was that was the light or the presence, but it felt like the ground of being, out of which everything comes and to which it all returns. I do not know. These were just the words that I used for it afterwards. Really what it was, was completely indescribable and as a result I have never really liked talking about it. I do not know how long it lasted, but then I was back, sitting on the floor. Everything appeared in some sense the same, but in another was utterly transformed. I got up and went out into the street, feeling a bursting sense of joy and well-being such as I had never felt before. Everything looked quite extraordinary. It was as if someone had turned up a dimmer switch and all the colours were brighter. Everything just glowed and seemed to radiate a kind of wondrous vibrancy. The buildings, shops, cafes, the people, the lamp posts, the pavement, it was all the same, radiant and technicoloured. I do not know how long it lasted, but eventually it faded. After that, however, the feeling of anguish never came back.

The glowing technicoloured experience of everything did fade with time, but what it arose out of never completely disappeared. Before that morning in Paris I had lived for years with a profound sense of apartness and aloneness, a sense of being separate from everything else with the chronic sense of lack that came with that. What arose out of whatever happened when I was sitting on the floor in Paris, and remained after all the technicolour had faded, was a sense that I was not really separate from everything else and nor was everything else really separate from anything else either, because really everything was one. Everything that appeared to be in the world, people, animals, plants, rocks and all the man-made stuff, though it seemed to be a collection of separate objects, was really, somehow a single unified whole. Only 'somehow', because I was aware that this was ultimately a mystery that I did not pretend to understand at all. But the sense that things are not really as they appear to be – that is separate and apart from each other – and that really there is only oneness became for me a certitude.

For me, the proof that this was not just some delusional experience was grounded in the fact that the anguish that had beset me for eight years vanished, never to return. There had been other experiences before this, of such things as energy lines around everything, including cars and bad-tempered Parisian women, but they had generally come after a period of fasting and I had always dismissed those as the result of an over-stretched sensibility (it was not until many years later, when I heard other people speak of energy lines that I thought that maybe it was not all the result of not having eaten for several days). This experience however was different, because I had not been fasting or anything else particularly. Everything had been entirely ordinary. And yet this profound shift had arisen. Moreover, it felt like the most real thing that had ever happened. I felt more inclined to doubt everything else, than to doubt that.

I have called it an 'experience' but in some sense it was not one at all, because there was no sense of me being there at all and the normal understanding of an experience is that it is something that happens to an experiencer. In an experience, according to our normal understanding of it, there is experiencer and experienced, or subject and object. In what opened up that morning in Paris, however, there was neither subject nor object. The only thing was, and it seemed rather strange to think about it, but I could recall what had happened afterwards. So, something had been experienced, or somehow some kind of experience had arisen. It had not been a complete blank, but nor had it been an experience of the normal kind. I did not know how to understand it at all at the time, and it still seems mysterious. It was like the opening up of a dimension of reality beyond the limitations of experiencer and experienced, subject and object. But somehow something of it still registered.

What this oneness was I did not know, but what was clear was that it just was. It was not going anywhere, nor did it have any kind of 'higher purpose'. It just *was*. So, everything that was just was or, as I put it to myself, there is only 'what is' and 'whatever is, is'. One result of this is that it became clear that there is no morality really in the world. Morality is normative, about how things 'should' be in the world, as opposed to how they are. What now became clear was that everything just was the way it was, and that nothing 'should' be different from how it was, however much we might not like it. I came to see all morality as just a human construction designed to make life better for ourselves, a kind of gloss that we 'gild and stain' the world with, as Hume put it, and not part of the way the world actually is at all. Seeing this did not make it seem wrong to talk of 'right' or 'wrong', it just gave such talk a different meaning. It no longer seemed like something real, but more like something that people found useful, ultimately as a way of trying to make the world the way they wanted it to be.

Another thing that no longer seemed so real was the whole idea of free will and choice. I had been painting for the previous few years and through doing so it had become clear that 'I' did not paint, rather painting 'happened'. The details of this I eventually wrote up as a PhD thesis and published as a book, but the central realisation was that a painter did not 'choose' the precise colours that he used, or precisely how the brush was moved across the canvas nor how much paint it left behind and yet it was these sorts of things that gave rise to the finished painting. Each painter seemed to have their own preferred range of colours and tones, their preferred way of working light within a painting and of constructing a composition. And it was clear from my own experience that none of these things were chosen. Rather the painter was drawn by a sensuous interaction with the painting surface into reworking the painting, changing things to remove things that were felt not to work until eventually a point was reached where nothing was felt to need changing and the painting was finished. So much of what made up the finished painting was the result of things that the painter does not choose or even decide on, that it seemed wrong to think of painting as something a painter did. Instead it seemed clear that it was something that actually just happened.

And what was true in painting was also clearly true in so much else in life. I was old enough, even by then, to be able to see that things that I believed I was choosing to do were in fact happening for reasons that I had little or no idea about. I had already done various things, thinking that I knew what I was doing and why I was doing them, only to realise later that they amounted to something very different from what I imagined at the time and that I had been motivated by factors of which I had been largely unconscious.

This was particularly true in relation to the glimpse, or minor awakening, that had happened, for so I came to understand it many years later. It was obvious that I had done nothing to make it happen. If anything had brought it on it was precisely the giving up on trying to run away from the anguish, which was brought on by complete despair. But I had not chosen to feel despair, I knew that. It had been genuine despair, a kind of letting go whatever the consequences. But just as I had not chosen to despair, nor had I chosen to give up and stop running away and instead to let go. It had all just happened.

What this also meant, however, was that there was nothing, absolutely nothing, that I could do to bring about another opening up to 'that' whatever it was. On one level, after that glimpse, all I ever wanted was for whatever it was to return. At the same time, however, I knew that there was nothing I could do to bring it about. So, seeking, or trying to get back to that place, was no more possible than seeking to just 'be' had ever been. I no longer felt like an atomistic individual, cut off and alone, with the anguish that that had brought on, which is what had prevented any form of 'spiritual' seeking before. Now that was gone, and there was a relative sense of belonging and well being. But because the way that it had gone was not because of anything that I had done, it was also clear that I could not do anything that would make what had opened up sitting on the floor that morning in Paris come back again.

Chapter Two

Knowing and Unknowing

A Known World

Human beings live in a world of knowing. We know, or think we know, who we and other people are. We know what things are and how they are related; that 'this' is a jug and 'that' a mat and that the jug is on the mat, on a table, in front of the window. The whole world of our experience is for us a known world, laid out in front of us without any sense of mystery about it. Everything just is what it is and all we have to do is to open our eyes and we see it for how it is. Reality is just as we perceive it to be. Moreover, it never seems to change; the jug today looks the same as the jug yesterday and tomorrow it will look the same again, because – we believe – it is the same jug. Everything within the world of experience appears like that, straightforward and immediately knowable. Things that are outside of the world of experience, however, are also experienced as known, just in a different way. We have a vast practical know-how. We know where things are, how they work, how to use them so they do what we want them to do, how to get to wherever we want to get to, in short, how to make our lives work as we want them to. Beyond that practical know-how we have a vast array of factual knowledge that we know because we have been told it or read it in a book or a newspaper, or seen it on the television, for instance, who is the Prime

Minister, what the capital of China is, or what is the structure of a plant cell. On a day-to-day level we also live in a world of knowing. We know what we did yesterday, what we are going to do today and what we will probably do tomorrow. We also know how we will do all these things; how we will get to work, do the things that we have to do there, cook dinner when we get home and later distract ourselves with what we know will be on television.

Knowing all these things enables us to pursue our purposes much more effectively. Whatever we want to do we can use this vast accumulated knowledge to do it. Human beings are extremely efficient at getting things done and knowledge is probably the most important tool that we use to make it possible. It is no wonder that the gaining of knowledge has so much status in our society and that we spend so much time and money educating our children.

I was brought up in this culture like everyone else and accepted it unthinkingly. Indeed, there did not seem to be anything to think about because the world as far as I was concerned for many years just was the way it seemed to be. I was also naturally curious and loved reading, especially history books. But at some point something else began to open up. I began to experience what I was taught at school and later at university as deadening, particularly science with its tendency to reduce one thing to another or explain one thing in terms of another. I had a strong sense that something, something rather massive, was being lost. The world of knowledge appeared to be quite definite and determinate, while the actual world of my experience seemed to have an openness and mystery about it. It was as if knowing things somehow seemed to change them. I did not understand this at the time, but felt it quite acutely.

I remember once walking up the hill from where I lived. It was just an ordinary London street, full of cars, with a pavement and a high Victorian wall at the side of the pavement holding back an embankment with trees and other plants growing upon it. Something about it made me stop and I just stood there for a while. There was something about everything there, the pavement I was standing on, the old wall to the side with trees and other plants above, that somehow was beyond anything that anyone could ever say, or know, about it. I felt that everything that meant anything to me was there, but in a way that I could not grasp or put into words, and which certainly could not be known. After this first time, this kind of experience of things as somehow ungraspable or unknowable came back more and more often. I did not really understand it, but what did seem clear to me was that the whole world of institutionalised knowledge, in particular science, with its abstracting, reducing and explanatory procedures, was somehow the denial of this. Somehow, the labelling of things and the turning of them into objects of knowledge seemed to change them, eliminating their inherent mystery and indeterminacy and turning them instead into something that seemed clear and determinate. It was this that more and more alienated me from the whole process of academic learning. So far from seeming like an education, it seemed like an indoctrination that took me away from what felt most real and true to me. Perhaps inevitably, I ended up dropping out of first school and later university.

During these years, I was also struggling with the sense of the meaninglessness of the whole cycle of becoming and self-seeking, which made doing most things rather difficult. The one thing that I did feel able to do was to seek after the truth, because that at that time did not seem to me to be about the self trying to get something for itself. Somehow, it always seemed more impersonal than that. The truth, I believed, was what it was, it was just a question of discovering what it was. There was no guarantee that whatever it was it would make the self feel better. What I was sure of though was that the world of institutionalised knowledge, for instance, universities and scientific research establishments, had somehow got it wrong. Their pretensions to knowledge, I believed, were somehow groundless or at least fundamentally exaggerated, distorting how things actually were.

I also believed that I might find an answer to the predicament I found myself in, not in the form of something that could be known, but precisely the opposite, in an understanding of things that made it clear how the intellectual world had gone wrong – that things could not be understood in terms of the known, that is as 'facts' that were 'true'. But, I think that because of the nature of my conditioning I still felt the need to try to understand this intellectually. It was something of a contradiction, but I did not see it at the time. So I started reading books on anything and everything that I could find. I read voraciously in philosophy, religion, anthropology, psychology, sociology, history, politics and literature. For several years I did little but read. By the end I was quite well read, and with a little bit more insight, but my basic experience of life was largely unchanged. I still believed that the institutionalised claims to knowledge were exaggerated but did not feel able to ground that in anything that seemed solid.

During these years, when most things brought on a sense of anguish, the one thing that acted as a balm was painting. Whenever I felt completely despairing I would make my way to the National Gallery and sit for a few hours in front of one or two paintings. However bad I felt when I arrived I always left feeling elated and full of joy. There was something in the paintings, a kind of otherworldly beauty or perfection that reminded me of what I felt I had lost. Seeing it in the paintings reinforced the sense I had that everything was not really meaningless, it was simply that I had lost touch with what gave everything its real meaning. As the years went by this sense that I had somehow lost touch with something, something which could be found in and through painting, gradually became stronger until eventually I abandoned my academic studies completely, moved to Paris and started painting myself. In painting I found a form of refuge from the anguish of self-seeking. Painting was a strict master and soon taught me that it worked better the less that 'I' was there trying to make it go in a certain direction. It was not an easy thing to do, because something within me constantly wanted to interfere in order to try to control the whole process. But over time I learned to keep that voice in check and to allow the work to happen largely in the way that it needed to according to some kind of internal logic. In painting, therefore, I found a temporary refuge from the constant cycle of self-seeking.

Most of my work at the time was figurative, working from still lives or landscapes. I would spend hour upon hour staring at the same objects in the room where I worked. Over time I gradually became aware that these same objects could appear very differently depending on how I looked at them. If I focused on the way the object was lit the tonal relationships would become accentuated, while the colours would seem to shrink back and almost disappear. At a later time, when I was working much more in terms of colour and therefore looking at things in this way, I noticed that the tonal relationships seemed to almost disappear; the whole becoming a kind of flattened out mosaic of colour. I also came to notice that after I had been working for several hours and then finally stopped, or if I took a break, everything around would look quite different to how it usually did. If I had been working in colour then the colours of everything around me seemed to be accentuated, while their tonal qualities would look muted compared to how they normally looked. On the other hand, if I had been working more in terms of light, the tonal relationships of everything afterwards would seem pronounced compared to how they usually looked, while their colours would seem muted. It was as if a different world had opened up each time, one that corresponded to how I had been working. This made me aware of the extent to which the world I experienced when I looked at it was the creation of the *way* that I looked at it.

I came to see that I did not see the world passively. Instead, I created it, in part at least, through the way I engaged with it. The world that I saw around me was not, therefore, just laid out in front of me, so that all I had to do was to open my eyes to see it as it was. Rather, my very way of engaging with it made it what it was for me. I became aware of myself 'creating' my world constantly as I went around. It seemed somewhat magical and mysterious at the same time.

To the extent that I was creating my own world, it also became clear that different creatures, with a different make up, would see a very different world. The world that human beings perceive is not 'natural' but the result of our particular make up and the way we engage in the world. For human beings, the world appears largely to consist of a collection of objects, each apart from the others, laid out before our gaze. We the perceiver are just another thing amongst them, although with a privileged status in that we can engage with them and manipulate them as we please. This way of seeing the world, as a collection of objects laid out in front of us, is useful to us as it provides us with a kind of background perception against which we can get on with what we are doing. Within this background perception everything appears to be just as I see and know it to be. A tree is simply a 'tree', a chair simply a 'chair'. There is nothing to search for or wonder at. This lack of mystery, the sense that everything I see is already known to me makes it easy for me to get on and do the things that I want to do. And that seems quite obviously the purpose of it all. Our senses have become adapted to enable us to survive and thrive in the world and they have succeeded to a high degree. We are in these terms the most successful creature ever to have lived on the planet. But, the more clearly I saw this, the more it was clear that this had all come at an enormous cost. Through the world appearing as a known world, the mystery of everything, that mystery which I had sometimes sensed and which had come back to the fore through my experience as a painter, was somehow lost.

This mystery was sometimes there now in ordinary life when I was not painting. It would sometimes appear in the most simple perception, for instance the way the shadow from a chair leg fell on the floorboards, or the texture of a simple thing, like a pot or a basket. But I also noticed that as soon as I became aware of it, it would seem to disappear. It took a while for me to be aware of how and why this seemed to happen. Eventually, I saw that the moment I became aware of this mysterious quality of things I would try and focus on it in order to keep hold of it, and somehow this seemed to make it go. The sense of mystery seemed only to appear in a gap within perception, as it were. If I tried to make it the focus for my attention, the object in perception, it would disappear. I found this frustrating and also despair inducing. It was as if something was playing a trick on me, dangling this in front of me and then withdrawing it as soon as I tried to grasp it.

As well as this sense of mystery what also became clear through painting was how much richer our visual experience is than we normally realise. I became aware that there were endlessly more tonal variations to things than I typically noticed, as well as endlessly more colours and variations of colour. So long as I was painting, and focussing on them, they were there, but once I stopped and resumed 'normal' life they would all also seem to fade away, or at least I would not notice them so much. It was as if in ordinary perception what is actually there is simplified, so that what is seen is only a fragment of what is really there, with the richness that became visible through painting largely absent. This left me with even more questions about the nature of reality, and especially the relationship between appearance and reality. Eventually, I left Paris, returned to England and the studies in philosophy that I had abandoned years earlier, to pursue these questions further.

Knowing

Within the Western tradition, perception is generally understood as a subject/object relationship. The person is the subject and what they see is the object. This subject/object relationship embodies the sense that the person has that he is real and so is everything else around him. This sense is not a belief, because it is not dispelled by just not believing it. Nor can it be dispelled by just wishing or willing it to go. Moreover, it does not seem to come and go, but seems constantly to be there, not so much as something within our experience as the single most powerful background determinant of all that does arise within it. As such, it seems to be part of the basic make up of human beings that they experience themselves as real people. For these reasons, this sense of being a real person can be understood to be a held-sense, one that conditions the whole nature of our experience. Within this experience, the subject experiences himself as a real 'person' and so the object, the tree, becomes for him a real 'tree'. That is to say, because the tree is experienced as being another real thing, alongside but separate from the person, it becomes for him an object. As a real and therefore separate object it is experienced as having real, determinate qualities. If it was experienced as having indeterminate qualities we would not be able to know it for what it was in the way that we do. Instead, it would be a vague thing, neither 'this' nor 'that'. It is therefore as determinate objects that the subject sees things and comes to know them. This is how the subject comes to see the tree as simply 'brown', missing the richness of colour, texture and tone that is actually there. It is because he knows it to be 'brown'. That is the word that he has learnt to subsume it under, thereby determining how it is seen. He has heard other people use that word for that kind of thing and learnt that it is the right word for the colour of a tree. And so that is all he sees. In other words, what the subject sees is a known reality, with what is known being the result of social conditioning and language.

This known world is what is seen from the perspective of a human being who experiences himself as a real person. For such a subject, everything is seen as being simply what it is known to be, only a 'tree' or only a 'chair'. That is to say, everything is perceived through the categories of knowledge and reduced to an expression of them. So, because a 'tree' is known to have a 'brown' trunk and branches that is what is seen. The 'known' world, then, is only a pallid version of what is actually there. In this known world the full richness of colours or tonal variations that are there are not seen, and the full richness of sounds that are heard are not registered. There is nothing for the subject to do about this, nothing that he can do to stop experiencing everything in this way, because anything that he does will only be another expression of the same subject/object way of experiencing everything and relating to it. The root of it is the held-sense within the body of the subject that he is a real person, for it is this that grounds the whole subject/object experience of reality. That held-sense can obviously not be dispelled by anything that the subject does, because anything and everything that he does is an expression of precisely that held-sense. This held-sense of oneself as a real person expresses itself as a grasping tendency towards whatever one encounters, so as to be able to possess it and use it to one's own advantage. This is typically how a 'person' relates to the things that he encounters, like tables, chairs, keys and door handles, as being mere objects for him to use so as to enable him to do the things that he wants to do. Another way in which this grasping tendency manifests is in trying to know reality, or rather in imposing a blanket of knowledge upon it. The world is not really known, but is experienced as if it is, through the imposition of the categories of knowledge upon it. This was why, when I glimpsed the mystery of the most simple thing in the interstices of perception it would vanish as soon as I tried to focus on it. The focussing was a form of grasping. It was me, the subject, trying to possess what I had glimpsed and thereby turn it into an object, so that I could have it, as the self always tries to do. I could not see it, however, because the mystery that it was could not be seen by a subject, someone who is seeing it as an object, for this way of looking at it is the denial of the very mystery.

It is this known quality of the experience of the subject, I came to realise, that makes it so unsatisfying. Everything is sensed to be only what it is known to be. As a result, nothing new is ever seen. Everything is familiar and so has a dull, stale quality. The practice of painting opened up a world of newness, through the enormous effort of focussing on the different qualities of things, for instance their colour or tone, rather than their 'thingness'. But as soon as I stopped painting, the ordinary subject/object relationship to everything would gradually return and with that the sense of everything as known, familiar and so dull.

This was also why, after the glimpse, or minor awakening, that occurred on the floor of my flat in Paris, everything appeared in technicolour. What was glimpsed was a reality that transcended the subject/object world. It was the reality that everything is really one and that the apparent separation of everything into subject and object is a delusion. With that perception came the temporary collapse of the held-sense of being a separate person, apart from everything else. And with that collapse the subject/object relationship to everything else collapsed too. Everything was no longer seen to be separate, to be a mere collection of objects, that made it all feel known and familiar. Instead, it all appeared to be new. Everything that I saw, even things or places that were entirely familiar, seemed completely fresh and new. And so everything seemed much brighter and more vibrant than it normally did. I remember particularly wandering around in the Place de la Bastille completely overwhelmed by the brightness and vitality that everything had. It was everything, the pavement, the buildings as well as the people walking around. Everything was in technicolour and more animate and alive than it normally seemed.

For several years before I moved to Paris I had a strong sense that how things really were was quite different from how they were taken to be in mainstream society. I did not understand how, but it had always seemed somehow obvious that a tree was not just a 'tree', and that instead it was something in a sense unknowable or mysterious. After the experience in Paris, this sense was much stronger. I did not understand what had happened in Paris, what it was or what it meant. All I did know was that nothing had ever felt so real. And this was reinforced by the falling away of the sense of the meaninglessness of everything and the anguish that that brought on. My not understanding what had happened, as well as the sense of profound mystery that had opened up, made me even more questioning of the forms of knowledge in the world, both those of ordinary life, but also of academia and science, because these were taken to be so straightforward. There seemed to be no mystery about what a 'tree' was, or the battle of Hastings, or evolutionary theory, or even the big bang from the way people would speak of them.

The more I looked at different claims to knowledge, however, whether in ordinary life, the various branches of science, history or social science the more insecure they actually seemed. What seemed apparent was that claims to knowledge worked pretty well within the domain within which they were originally made. But if one looked at what ultimately substantiated these claims they came to look like castles built upon foundations of sand. Each domain, or area of human functioning, I came to see as a kind of practice, for instance, botany, history, painting or even chess. Within each practice there were accepted criteria for what an acceptable knowledge claim amounts to. So, if someone within the practice, says or writes something that meets those criteria it is recognised as knowledge. But, for someone outside of the practice, these criteria can seem quite opaque and therefore the knowledge claims incomprehensible.

Furthermore, those criteria of what counts as knowledge within each practice are subject to revision from time to time. Typically, within any individual practice there is the dominant model of how to see and think about the world. If this dominant model starts to fail to account for the way things are over time, it can eventually be replaced by a new model.[1] This is a revision to the criteria of what constitutes knowledge within that domain. As a result, it is typically accompanied by the rejection of a lot of what had previously been considered knowledge and its replacement by a new set of beliefs based upon the newly dominant criteria or model. Classic examples of this kind of process are the histories of both astro-physics and art history.

The knowledge claims in these areas then are criteria or model based. They are not made directly. As such, they are conventional, or social, constructions because they are based on agreed models of how things are, or criteria of how to do things.

This replacement of one set of criteria by another is not seen in ordinary life. But knowledge claims in ordinary life are just as much based on social conventions and constructions. This can be seen by considering the simple distinction constantly made, and universally agreed upon, between chairs and tables. If we take a typical chair and a typical table and lengthen the legs of the chair by a millimetre whilst reducing its back also by a millimetre everyone would agree that it is still a chair. The same if we do it again, and again. However, if we carry on, we will reach a point where its legs will be the same length as the table's and it will have no more back to it. At which point, most people will probably say that it is no longer a chair but has become a table. At what point, however, did this happen? At each point we only lengthened the legs by a millimetre whilst lowering the back by the same amount. Such a change is negligible. So, there is no clear point at which it ceased to be a chair and became a table. What this shows is that there is no clear class of things that are tables and another that are chairs. Rather it is a matter of conventional usage that we call 'these' things chairs and 'those' tables.

---

[1] T. Kuhn. *The structure of scientific revolutions.*

This is true not just for tables and chairs but for all concepts. There are no straight lines between 'different' things. Instead, what makes something a 'this' or a 'that' is a matter of convention, of how human beings have decided to slice up the world for their own convenience.

This goes against how we normally think. We think that certain things just are chairs and others just are tables. We do not normally think about it but, if pressed, we will probably try to point to certain criteria that make some things chairs and others tables. For instance, someone might say that a chair is something with four legs, a seat to sit on and a back. But, then what about office chairs which often have only one leg, with a number of rollers under a flat base and which tilt? That does not fit the definition, but we still recognise it as a chair. We can try to accommodate this by making the definition less precise, for instance by saying that a chair is a seat for one with legs of some sort. But this does not work, because it will still not encompass things like bean bags. And if we try to get round this by broadening the definition still further, for instance saying that it is a 'portable seat for one' it will now include not just the things we recognise as chairs, but also things like bicycle seats as well.[2] It becomes clear that there will not be a single set of criteria that captures all and only those things that we call chairs, which is what a defining set of criteria needs to do.

Moreover, what a chair is, is something that can only be understood through its relationships with other items of furniture, for instance, tables, desks, stools and benches, as well as the various and differentiated uses that we make of them within the different practices that make up our lives. Chairs, for example, are what we sit on when eating dinner at the table, or when we are at work in the office. What this means is that something is only a 'chair' because of the wider practical context of our lives, that is to say the various practices, within which 'chairs' show up, and in its turn this wider

---

[2]H. Dreyfuss. *Being-in-the-world*. A commentary on part 1 of Heidegger's *Being and Time*.

practical context can itself only be understood in relation to the existence of other practices and so on. Thus, for example, sitting on a chair in the office only arises because of the wider context of business, modern economics and the transport links that enable people to get to work. So far from a thing like a 'chair' being knowable in isolation as a determinate object what we actually find then is that it can only be understood for what it is in relation to its place within a web of inter-related practices that takes in the whole of our lives. In other words, all we have is simply a way of going on, or behaving, within a set of inter-related practices and all of this cannot be reduced to something determinate like a definition. So, in answer to the question, 'what is a chair?' all we can say is that 'these' are the things that we call chairs, because that is how we use them. Nothing more, ultimately, can be said to substantiate it.

Knowledge claims, then, are conventionally accepted assertions made on the basis of agreed criteria, whether these criteria are explicitly articulated, simply assumed or whether they are merely an accepted way of 'going on'. All of these knowledge claims have as their raison d'être that they support us in our attempts to survive and get on in the world. This is the real nature of knowledge. Gaining knowledge is something that humans do in order to gain power and control in the world, so as to be able to pursue our purposes as well as possible. Knowledge, then, is tied in with the constant striving of the self to get something for itself. It is instrumental in that struggle and highly effective. But it comes at a price. The human tendency to 'know' its environment means that people live, as it were, semi-detached from everything around them. The inherent mystery of everything is lost and instead everything seems prosaic and dull. A tree and a chair are just that, a mere 'tree' and a mere 'chair', familiar and known and hence in a way dead to us.

Despite all this seeming quite clear, there was something in me that could not live this, could not let go to not knowing things. I felt drawn to try to show – through studying and eventually writing a book – that this was how things were; that reality could not really be known and that what could be known was limited and a lot less important, or meaningful, than what it left out. In a way, I wanted to know the unknowability of things and could not see the contradiction. I do not think that it is a meaningless or impossible task to try to show the limits of knowledge; it has been done by philosophers from Kant to Merleau-Ponty. But to argue for it and try to establish it is still to remain within the world of knowing, when really what I was sensing and reaching for was the living of unknowing and that is something of a completely different order to the intellectual demonstration of the intrinsic limitations of rationality and knowledge. For many, many years I could not, or would not, see this. I felt that it was important to try to establish the limits of knowing in order to avoid the charge that unknowing was only a kind of soft-headed fantasy, a form of self-indulgence that I held to simply because it made me feel better. Now, I realise that this was a wrong turn, as it were. I think that in many experiences within ordinary life, as well as in the world of experience that painting opened up, I had got to the edge of knowing, or the door of unknowing as it were, and instead of letting go I had turned back towards knowing or trying to know. Something of my basic make up as well as my conditioning, the academic family that I came from, the school and university education that I had received, or the general prejudice in favour of 'intellectualism' in Western society, made me unable to let go. Something in me could not trust the realm of unknowing that is so constantly, but obliquely, present. Needing to 'know' I turned my back on it and went back to book learning and the attempt to know. I do not think that this is a particularly unusual experience. Many people, I believe, reach a similar place only to turn away.

Pax Lodge

Many years later I found *The Open Secret* by Tony Parsons in a bookshop. It was a revelation. So much of what he said chimed with things I had experienced before or felt I had known all my life. But there were other things that he spoke of that I had never thought of in that way before, particularly the delusional nature of the whole sense of being a person. As with many other people, I think that I had had some kind of intuition of this when I was much younger but, because everybody else around me seemed to feel that they were a real person in a quite unproblematic way, I assumed that the problem was some how to do with me. A few years after finding the book I started going to meetings. I was not looking to become enlightened. I had long since given up on believing in such a thing. But I found in Tony's words something that I had not felt for so, so many years, a sense of real belonging, of home. I had gone so far in another direction for so long, however, that it took a while for it to percolate through. I carried on going to meetings and had a sense as time went on that something was gradually shifting within, I know not how. It was like a kaleidoscope being gradually turned back into focus. At first it was more of an intellectual, clarifying of ideas and how they relate, but gradually it became something else, more a way of being that was changing. Something still felt 'out of place' as it were, but there was a clear sense of having found again what I had always known to be true.

After about three years, when I was at one of the meetings at Pax Lodge in Hampstead, someone asked Tony a question and as part of his reply he said, 'this is about absolute unknowing'. As soon as he did so, I felt something shift within me. It was quite physical, like something moving and clunking into place. Nothing else happened and nothing seemed to change. The meeting carried on and I carried on sitting there and everything was apparently the same. But then, a couple of days later, when I was walking in the street up the road from where I live the things I saw started, as it were, to glow. All the most ordinary things, the leaves on the trees, the tarmac pavement, even the chewing gum trodden into the pavement and the litter, began to take on a kind of radiant quality which it is impossible to describe. For the first couple of days I was a bit anxious that it might go, but it did not and it soon became clear that it was not going to. Instead it has slowly filled out, until eventually it has become a constant presence.

When I thought later about how this happened, it was clear that at the time when I heard Tony say 'this is about absolute unknowing' what occurred was something like a letting go to this, or acceptance of it. For the whole of my adult life I had been caught up in the thrall of knowing, of needing to know. In a way, it had been the deepest drive in my life, somehow to 'know' this, the answer to all this. When Tony said those words, it was like being presented with the suggestion that I never could, or would, know the answer, that the answer could not be known, that it lay precisely outside of the realm of knowledge and knowing. For some reason, instead of resisting that possibility, something inside me just said 'alright' to it. It was like giving up a struggle against something and just letting it be, not trying to control a situation to make it as I needed it to be, but instead just allowing it to be as it is. For me, knowing the answer to life, to the riddle of existence, had always been the great compensation for everything. My life had been relatively hard, my health had not been great since I left Paris, in worldly terms my life was something of a failure and disappointment to those who loved me and I knew that in worldly terms I had 'not fulfilled' my potential. But knowing, I believed, was going to make up for all that. If I could only know the answer I would have, as it were, the compensation for it all. I was like a gambler who had sold everything they had in order to place one great bet and had placed it all on one number coming up. It was a bit like my whole life was staked on this. And now Tony was saying that this dream I had of knowing the answer somehow could never be fulfilled and something in me just said 'alright then'. It was like jumping into a void, not knowing what was there. Perhaps that is precisely what 'unknowing' means.

Does that mean that my 'letting go' caused a kind of unknowing awareness or experience to open up? And does that mean that for unknowing to happen a kind of surrender, or letting go, to it has to occur? That would be the temptation and it is a conclusion that is typically drawn. It fits with our assumptions about the world and how things come to pass. We think that rain causes the plants to grow and that putting the kettle on causes the water to boil and that it is because we choose to do what we do that it happens. In the same way, my letting go would seem to have caused this shift in experience. This, however, is to misunderstand what actually occurred and how these things arise in general. For a start, 'I' did not let go. It just happened. Just as in Paris, where I did not choose to despair or choose to stop running away from the sense of anguish, I did not choose, when Tony said those words, to accept not to know the answer and to let go. It was very clear at the time: it was just something that happened. Secondly, even if I wanted to let go, I could not. The self cannot let go. The very existence of the sense of self gives rise to a sense of something being missing or lacking which then in turn leads to grasping or the pushing and pulling of the world in order to try to make good that sense of lack. Knowing is one way by which this grasping tendency of the self manifests itself. The self always tries to know, so that it can gain control of where it thinks it is, which will enable it, it thinks, to pursue its purpose of trying to make things better for itself more effectively. So, the self does not allow unknowing to be. This was why, when I was younger, often when I was painting, and a sense of mystery would appear in a very ordinary perception of something, I noticed there was always a movement to get hold of it, or grasp it, to try to know it. And then it would immediately disappear. This is how the self functions. It tries to know everything it comes across. So, it could never accept unknowing, or let go to it. To let go to unknowing, then, is not just to accept not to know the answer, it is in a way the letting go of the whole structure of the self, the grasping, knowing, pushing and pulling relation to the world. At least, that is how it was for me, because knowing was so central to the structure of the way my self functioned.

So long as there is the expression of the sense of a self, therefore, there will only ever be grasping and movement towards something. Letting go to unknowing, then, only happens when the self gives up. But obviously, giving up is not something that the self can do, for everything that the self does is done to try to gain something for itself. So, if the self tried to let go, it would only be doing so because it thought that by doing so it would get something for itself. In which case, it would not really be a form of letting go at all, but actually of grasping, or of trying to pull something towards itself. This was what my asceticism had been for years and why it was doomed to failure. Letting go, then, can only ever be something that happens, never something that a self, or person, does. Therefore, the idea that someone needs to try to 'let go' in order to get to a place of unknowing could not be more confused.

Furthermore, even if it is understood that there is no separate person with free will and choice who can decide to let go, the whole idea that unknowing arises because letting go happens is a misunderstanding of the way in which things actually arise. It presupposes a linear picture of causation, according to which x causes y, and this is just another story, or thought-construction, that people tend to tell themselves. In reality, it is not simply the rain that causes the plants to grow. It is rather a whole collection of circumstances, including the rain, but also the sun, the warmth, the soil, the nutrients in the soil, the degree of shelter the plant has, the in-built growth potential of the seeds and so on. All of these factors are themselves tied in with a whole range of other features. For instance, the rain is connected to the level of cloud formation and that to the level of pressure in the atmosphere and so on and so on. Ultimately, there only is the totality of what is happening at that moment, all of which results from the totality of everything that happened the moment before and so on. The letting go is, then, no more the cause of the movement into unknowing than is the change in the level of pressure in the atmosphere. And the change in the level of pressure in the atmosphere is no more the cause of the plants growing than is the letting go. There is only the totality of 'what is' and that brings about whatever then *is* as an ensemble. No single thing causes any other single thing.

The idea that one thing causes another is an abstraction, or construction, out of thought that the self imposes on 'what is' to make sense of it for itself, to enable itself to get by in the world. Thought is a kind of picture of things. It can be a picture about the present, in the form of a simplification, turning the entirety of what is arising into a narrative that pares it down to something relatively simple and schematic, for instance, that so and so has just got home, or that the weather is cold today. Alternatively, thought can be a picture of the past, in the form of a memory, again typically a pared down narrative of what happened. Or it can be a picture of a possible future, as a kind of fantasy. Or it can be a picture of a normative reality, an emotional reaction/assertion about how reality 'should' be as opposed to how it actually is.   In relation to all these different time dimensions one of the most common pictures that human thought presents are pictures about causal relationships between elements in the world. This kind of thinking is something that human beings do almost continually, creating an abstraction out of the whole of everything, the 'what is' that is our actual inherence, in the form of a picture of how this whole is structured. This causal picture is always incomplete, however, because in reality causal relations are never in the linear form of x causes y, but something infinitely more complex and holistic. To enable us to function in the world then we operate with a massively simplified and abstracted picture of causation. This linear causal thinking, and all the linear causal stories that we construct for ourselves, gives humans great power through giving them the means of controlling and manipulating their environment to their own ends. Again, though, it does so at the price of removing them from the natural reality of 'what is'.

Unknowing

It was this natural reality that began to reveal itself in the few days after the afternoon in Pax Lodge. The most evident feature of it was a sense of the wondrousness of everything. In a way, this was similar to the technicoloured world that opened up after the awakening in Paris, in that everything seemed so much more alive than it usually did.   But it was a lot more subtle.   Like any experiential quality, it is hard to describe this wondrousness. The closest thing to say would be that everything had an extraordinary softness about it, and still does. It also had more of a mysterious quality. It was like the mystery of being, the mystery that things just *are*, and how they appear in their beingness moment by moment, as it were. To see this natural reality is to see something that looks endlessly new as if it has never been seen before. This is because, in truth, it has not. Whatever is seen or sensed moment by moment is, in reality, endlessly fresh and new. It is only because things are seen normally by a person through the prism of knowing that this freshness is not seen. Thus, when a person looks at something, like the jug on the table, what is seen is not the jug as it actually is, which is a thing that he has never seen before, but the jug that he knows to be there, the known 'jug'. This known jug is a construction out of memory, the memory of the jug as it was yesterday and the day before and the day before that. It is something entirely familiar, because what it actually is, is the memory or thought that the person already has of it. This is superimposed on 'what is', the appearance that is actually in front of him, so what he sees is not something fresh and new, which is what it actually is, but something remembered or 'known'. Hence, its grey, familiar, somewhat dull and unsatisfying quality.

The more I came to see this, the more I came to realise that all thoughts are actually untrue. The thing referred to as 'the jug' is quite different from a thought about it. It is not just that one is 'physical' while the other is 'mental' it is that the latter does not correspond to the former in the way that we tend to assume that it does. Thoughts are a picture of reality, they are not reality itself. And any picture must transform the nature of what it pictures in order to be able to picture it. This needs a qualification. To say that thoughts are not reality themselves is not literally true. They are real, in terms of what they are themselves, just in the same way that the jug is, or the litter in the street, but their content, the pictures they contain of things, are not. The realm of thought, then, is the realm of a constructed reality. The constructions that it pictures to us are useful in terms of enabling us to get around in the world to achieve our purposes, but they do so by reinforcing our sense of separation from everything that is part of the human condition.

This is not to say that there is anything wrong with thought. Thought just happens, the same as everything else and is neither intrinsically good nor bad. Nor am I saying that in any way people should try to resist thought, or not live in thought. The very idea of that is itself just another thought. And to try to live it would only be to reinforce thought, for it would be to live out the idea that this thought, the thought that resisting thought and trying not to live in it, is somehow 'better' than doing the opposite. And that is precisely how the thrall of thought maintains its hold on us. It is another facet of the same paradox that if the self sees the emptiness and futility of self-seeking and so tries to stop doing it, that itself is just another expression of precisely the movement that it is supposedly wanting to stop.

So, this is not a message against thought. Rather it is simply an attempt to reveal the nature of thought and the role that it plays in the life of human beings. Thought is an incredibly powerful tool for the grasping and manipulation of features of the world. But it comes at the cost of alienating us from our original inherence, which is the world of unknowing. Thought presents a known world, when 'what is' is unknown and unknowable.

We have seen that the ordinary experience of human beings is fundamentally oriented around our practical purposes. We relate to things in terms of *what* they are, a jug, a table, a car, a traffic light and that enables us to get on, pursuing our purposes in relation to them. *That* they are, we do not see. The miracle of being, the miracle that everything *is*, is somehow overlooked. We look straight past the endless miracle of beingness unfolding around us, so much are we in a hurry to get to where we are trying to go.

When things are seen for what they really are, a manifestation beyond all knowing, there is a kind of stopping. The 'known' world is tied in with our sense of becoming, our trying to get to a 'better' place. It is in this mode that we spend almost all our lives, trying to do this, get that, achieve something else. We are always on the move *to* somewhere. This movement is grounded upon our basic experience of something being missing or lacking and needing to do something to make up for the lack, but it is also based on our experience of the world as a known world. When that ceases, when the sense that everything we see or hear is already known to us stops, the whole structure of becoming slows down and stops with it. This stopping happens because we need already to know what something is if we are to be able to use it to try to get ourselves to a 'better' place, and in unknowing experience we do not have that sense that we know what everything already is. Instead, there is a sense of mystery and of something unknown or beyond knowing. And, with that, a natural stopping occurs.

Out of this stopping what could be described as a form of contemplation of 'what is' arises equally naturally. In this contemplation, things no longer appear to be what we know them to be. Instead, all that is left could be described as the beingness of the unknown. Even this is not right, though, as it seems to point towards a determinate quality, when precisely what is seen is the indeterminacy of a mystery. Also, beingness seems to point towards the beingness of some *thing*, for instance, a glass or a jug. But these are objects in the known world and it is not the beingness of one of those that is seen. Rather, it is almost the opposite, the emptying out of the sense that some thing is really some *thing* at all, for instance, a glass, or a jug; it is the emptying out of particular being so that all that is left is beingness itself. What is then left is a kind of presence. This presence is not the presence of an object, or even a thing, like a jug, or a glass. Instead, it is more like the presence of something entirely other *as* a jug. The jug is simply the form in which this presence appears.

When the world is seen in this way it appears just to *be*, and in its is-ness there is no meaning, or purpose, no sense of what it is for, or what could be done with it. To see the world in this way is to be in a place of unknowing and that is to be back in a similar place to the place of the small child looking out onto the world not knowing what it sees. Out of this unknowing arises the sense of wonder that the small child experiences and which returns when we no longer 'know' the world.

To realise that one does not know is humbling, and out of the place of unknowing a sense of humility arises, a soft humility. Here we know that we know nothing and in a sense are nothing, for the same empty presence that is in everything else we find in ourselves too. This again arises quite naturally because we and our experience are not two things, but different aspects of the same phenomena. In subject/object experience the nature of the subject and the nature of the object are two sides of the same coin, and it is the same in what can be called unknowing experience. From a place of unknowing the claim to know seems deluded, like the expression of a power-crazed person. In the experience of unknowing what arises seems to have a limitless and unconditional value, yet it is not something that I can have or control. To seek this control is to turn one's back on all that is most precious. Yes, it increases our sense of power and security, but does so at the cost of estranging us from everything that we ever really wanted.

The sense of knowing nothing and of being nothing also creates a sense of poverty. It is the poverty of having nothing. It is the opposite of the sense of being wealthy, both inwardly and outwardly, that comes with a knowing relation to things. This wealth is an unsatisfying wealth, however, for it comes with the sense of being separate from everything that is known, which gives rise to an experience of lack that is intrinsically unsatisfying. In the absence of a sense of knowing there is no such separation and hence no sense of lack. With the experience of unknowing, then, comes the beginning of a sense of wholeness and of 'what is' being enough just as it is.

Ordinary experience, we have seen, is subject/object. It is based on the sense that 'I' am real and therefore so is everything else. In unknowing experience, this sense that everything is real is absent. What is seen is not an object, or collection of objects, but something unknown, a mystery. As a mystery it has an indeterminacy that means it is experienced very differently to an object, the nature of which is both real and determinate. The way an object is seen arises in part out of everything being seen through the lens of memory. It is because I remember that this is a jug, the same jug that was here yesterday and the day before, that I see it is a mere jug now and why it feels so dull and unsatisfying. In unknowing experience this seeing of everything through the lens of memory is significantly absent, leading everything to seem fresh and new. This is not black and white, however, for if there was no memory, no contrasting of present experience with what is remembered from the past, there would only be the innocent wonder of the small child as they experience the world for the first time. And this is not how it is. There is still a form of recognition, the glass is still recognisably a glass, the tree a tree. There is not a complete blank as when we look at something that we have never experienced before. But there is a sense of freshness, presence and mystery that is quite different from ordinary experience. The experience of unknowing, then, is like the wonder of small children, but it is not it.

Because what is seen in unknowing is still recognised, the glass is still a glass, it is still a form of experience or awareness. It is only when this awareness becomes self-conscious, which typically involves the attempt to grasp at what arises in experience, that knowing returns. The self is not able just to see something for what it is but will always try to grasp whatever it is for itself. In the realm of perception that means the transformation of something open and unknowable into something known and so closed. The grasping at experience by the self, however constant it may appear to be, is not necessary and nor is it the only form of relationship to things that is possible. Unknowing awareness, in which the palpable mystery and wonder of things remains just that, is also possible. So, there can be both a knowing awareness and an unknowing awareness.

The sense of wondrousness that arises in unknowing naturally leads to silence, for what is seen is beyond all possible words and so beyond communication. The unknown glass cannot be described. It is a kind of presence and in that presence is a palpable mystery. To reach for it in any way is to lose it. But if the unknown glass cannot be described and that is what is really there, to what then does the word 'glass' refer?

This question rests on a basic confusion. Words like 'glass', or 'yellow' seem to have a meaning all by themselves, in this case to refer to glass and yellowness. This can give rise to the belief that they and all words have this meaning or referring capacity within themselves. It is clear, though, that other words, like 'even' or, 'so', or 'consequently' do not have a meaning by themselves, but only within the context of a whole sentence. Moreover, even words like 'glass' or 'yellow' do not really have a meaning or reference by themselves. Some things are only yellow because others are blue or red. And some things are glass only because others are wood, or metal. That is to say, the meaning of all words is only given in contrast to the meaning of other words. Words, therefore, do not have a meaning by themselves, but only in relation to other words and in the context of sentences. From this it is clear that language is intrinsically dualistic, in that all meaning within it only arises through the contrast and distinction between things as different from each other.

A similar argument can be applied to the contention that meaning does not reside in individual words, but in sentences. A sentence like 'snow is white' seems to have a meaning all by itself, but if what 'white' means can only be understood in relation to what 'yellow', 'red' and 'blue' mean then clearly it does not. The same is true for all other words and sentences. So far, then, from individual words or sentences having a meaning by themselves the locus of meaning for language is the whole of language itself. Rather than trying to understand language by trying to understand the particular meaning of individual words, or sentences, we need to understand the meaning of words and sentences through an understanding of language as a whole.

Language is a tool that humans use to communicate with each other in order to get things done. When we say things like 'pass the butter', or ask 'how did you get on today?' we are doing something, in order to pursue a purpose we have, and using words to do it. It is the same when we say something like 'It is raining'. This is primarily a communication to someone, to inform them about something that might be significant, and only secondarily a reference to a feature of the world. The referential feature of this sentence, so far from being the locus and ground of its meaning, as traditional Western philosophy would believe, is actually only an abstraction out of what it primarily is, which is a purposeful communication, the doing of something. The clearest examples of the use of language to do something are what J.L. Austin called 'performatives', sentences that are uttered in particular contexts as a way of performing an action. Classic examples are, 'I hereby name this ship the ...' and 'I hereby declare you to be man and wife'. In these cases, the performing of the action, the naming of a ship or the marrying of two people, and the uttering of these sentences are one and the same thing. There is not the saying of one thing and the doing of something else. The utterances *are* the actions. What I am claiming is that all sentences actually are a form of performative, only less superficially obviously so than in these examples.

Another way of describing this is to say that language is not so much anchored to a pre-existing world as formative of it. It is not because snow is a real determinate substance in the world and whiteness a real determinate quality that we understand a sentence such as 'snow is white'. It is rather that we use words like 'snow' and 'white' in sentences like 'snow is white' to do and achieve things, because the doing of those things is useful to us. And this, in turn, contributes to the forming of our experience, in which 'snow' appears to be 'white'. Thought, however, does not see this, but instead abstracts out of this usage a real world containing real snow and real whiteness, which it then persuades us pre-exist this usage and are independent of it. But this is to turn the phenomenal reality on its head.

Language is able to perform its role as the medium for the performance of an array of actions in part because it is a construction, a construction by people, for people, to make worldly functioning easier. There is nothing natural or inevitable about language. As can be seen from the example of Eskimos having many words for snow, while English has only one, words are created to serve our purposes. Where no further distinctions are needed, none are made. So, there are an endless variety of hues of the colour green that can be seen in the world, if we are able to see them, but we have only a number of words for a few of them, for instance, bottle green, grass green and emerald green. Most of the shades of green simply have no name. They are still there, however, it is only that because we do not have words for them we tend not to notice them or see them so clearly or even be aware of them at all. Eskimos will see the different kinds of snow, for which they have words, far more clearly than will an English person, who does not.

The word 'glass' then does not gain it's meaning by direct reference to some feature in the world, but rather in a more indirect and complex way. First, it is part of a language network, in which it's meaning is given through the difference or contrast between it and other words. Second, it derives it's meaning from the use made of this language network by human beings in order to get things done in the world. Rather than referring to something in the world, it is part of the structure by means of which human beings categorise the world, so as to be able to manipulate it. This categorisation happens according to the needs and culture of the people concerned. Where more differentiation is needed there are more words, where less is needed there are less.

This ties in with the experience of the person that he is real and his world is real and that being real the world can be known. Language reinforces this 'known' world in various ways. For a start, we tend to experience the world in terms of the language that we use. So, because the thing in front of me is called a jug I tend to experience it as just a 'jug', that is as an example of the kind of object to which that label applies. Furthermore, as a tool for getting things done, language is part of the whole structure of becoming that forms the inherence of a person. In both these ways, the practice of using language is part of the structure that maintains the experience of a 'person' in the world.

Most thinking also happens in language. Language and thought, then, complement each other in the construction of the world in which the 'person' lives out their lives. Thought pictures the world and the way in which it does is linguistic. The same 'known' world is found in both, because they are both the expression of the same mode of experience. Living their life in thought and language reinforces for the human being the held-sense that they are a real 'person' and that everything else is real too. It thereby reinforces and sustains the whole world of the 'person' in which everything is known.

All of this is not to say that there is anything wrong with using language. It is another thing that simply happens. Language is as much a feature of the world as anything else. It is in part, though, through what is pictured in language that delusion arises; the sense human beings have that language really refers to things, that the things that it refers to are real and that by manipulating language, whether in speech or in thought, it is dealing with a real, known world. This is the dream world, the world of becoming, in which most human life is played out.

The held-sense that grounds the experience of a 'person' as a subject/object experience, with language and thought each presenting a known reality, together keep human beings in a world that they experience as separate from themselves. So long as experience arises in subject/object form this held-sense of separation from everything is always there, constantly and ubiquitously, so much so that it is not even seen. We only see something when it is different from something else. Something constantly present, forming the background to all our perceptions, all our experience, is not even seen or noticed. Experiencing ourselves as separate from everything around us makes it much easier and more practical to get things done in life. But it does so at the very high cost of removing us from the realm of our original inherence.

Once this sense of separation is pierced, however, what emerges is a world that no longer feels known and in which whatever arises no longer seems to have the same reality that it formerly did. This world is indescribable, beyond the dualistic categories of language. It cannot be said, it cannot be thought. Nor can it be owned or grasped. It is beyond the whole world of becoming. And therefore, it naturally gives rise to a silent wonder and contemplation.

Chapter Three

Awakening

What Happened

A few months after the weekend in Pax Lodge Tony held a retreat in Wales for a few days and I went. It was the first time I had been to such an event and did not know what to expect. I nearly went home after the first evening, as it all seemed too sociable for me, but eventually I decided to stay.

The first couple of days were pretty uneventful, but then I began to feel an enormous sense of joy and a vast, almost explosive, energy. I went to see a cousin of mine who lived not too far away and she described me as 'radiating well-being'. All the way back this sense of explosive energy was there making me drive stupidly fast and I ended up missing my turn of an A road because I was travelling so fast on the outside lane and could not get across quickly enough, something I have never done before. The next day, the energy was still there, but there was also a feeling of love for everybody and an impulse to embrace everyone. And yet it all felt completely natural. That night I was up late talking to the landlord of the B&B where I was staying and so went to sleep in the early hours. Only a short time later, I woke at 3.30 overcome with joy and laughing fit to burst. I did not know what I was laughing about, or why I felt such joy. It was just there. And over the next few hours it just got stronger and stronger. For a time there would just be this vast sense of joy, getting stronger and stronger, and then I would be overcome by uncontrollable laughter again. I seemed to find something almost unbearably funny, though I had no sense what it was. By around six in the morning, I was in what I can only describe as raptures of ecstasy or a kind of beatific joy. I cannot really describe what it was actually like, and it was completely different from any feeling I had ever known before in life. Nothing has ever been even remotely close to what arose that night. At some point I remember thinking that if it carried on much further I might go completely mad, and shortly after it began to subside.

A few hours later I began to be aware that everything felt like home. I did not really understand what home meant, there was just a sense that everything was it. Things did not look radiant, or technicoloured, as they had in Paris, or after Pax Lodge. There was just a sense of having come home again. I wondered, rather than worried, about whether it might end, not really believing that it would. There was something about it that made it feel irreversible.

The most obvious immediate change was that the vast energy that was there just before continued to be there. I continued to wake at 3.30-4 for weeks after coming back from Wales and did not feel tired. I simply could not sleep any more. I would try, but it was useless, so I would end up getting up in the middle of what had previously been the night. The other way in which the sense of being full of energy came out most strongly continued to be when I was driving. I felt pushed to drive really fast, in a way that I had never done before, and for a very long time driving a lot faster than the speed limit became normal and seemingly irresistible.

The other most evident change that was immediately apparent was that having finally come back home it was clear that seeking was over for me. I had had a strong sense of being on a journey for many, many years, right back to when I was fifteen and it was suddenly clear that all of that was over. I felt that I had somehow come full circle and returned to where I had been before it all began. It was an odd feeling, not unwelcome, but strange. I could see how much of everything that had been going on for me for years had been to do with this journey and it felt extraordinary in a way that it was suddenly over. Not extraordinary, in the sense of it being an event of any great significance, but simply that having done something for so, so long, for it suddenly to end, literally overnight, felt rather extraordinary. I realised that I had never really imagined that it would ever end. I had always been something of a sceptic about the idea of people waking up. It was not something I had ever really believed in and certainly not something that I had ever really sought for myself or imagined might happen. When I had previously heard Tony talk about awakening or liberation, it was not something that I thought would happen, or particularly wanted to happen. I wanted the residual sense of not-being-home to go, that sense of being apart from everything, but having lived with it for so many years I did not imagine that it ever could or would. Nor, strangely, had I connected up the ending of the sense of not-being-home which I wanted, with what Tony was calling awakening, which I never really imagined could happen. Now I see that the two are exactly the same thing. But at the time, I think there was still part of me that saw talk of awakening or liberation as just more self-seeking and tied up with pretensions to 'enlightenment' and some kind of esoteric state, and so something in me rejected it. For all these reasons, I had assumed that I would always be a seeker and it was only now, when seeking stopped, that I realised how much of my held-identity had been constructed around this search.

Other facets of my held-identity also seemed to disappear at this time. There were things that I had done for almost the whole of my life, and which I had always seen as part of who I was, which simply stopped overnight. For example, since I was a child I had always had a fascination with history. It had always been a passion throughout my life. I had read history books since before I can remember and at the time was in the middle of a book about the personal experience of ordinary people, from all countries and all sections of society, during the Second World War. I took it to Wales with me but did not look at it while I was there and have not picked it up again since. Nor have I felt any inclination to read anything else historical. My previous fascination with history now seems rather strange and I cannot really understand it, and certainly not how strong it was. Before, it had always been something of a fixture through all the stages of my life. Despite everything that had changed or happened, it had always been there, almost like a very old friend, who I could always go back to and pick up from where we had left off. And now it was just gone. It went overnight, but there was no sense of loss. It was simply gone, as if it had never been there. In that sense, it felt more like something that had been part of someone else, and not part of me, who I really was. So, the fact that it had gone did not seem to matter.

It was the same with museums. As with history, museums had been a great love of mine all my life since I was a child. My favourite place when I was small was the Natural History Museum in London. Then, as a teenager the National Gallery became a kind of second home to me and I am not sure I would have made it through those years without it being there and being able to go to it when I needed to. Later, throughout my adult life I have always liked to visit museums, both in London and wherever else I have gone. But this too now suddenly stopped. A few weeks after coming back from Wales a friend suggested going to the British Museum together. When we got there she asked me if there was anything I particularly wanted to see and I realised strangely that there was not. Previously, when I used to go to museums there was always a kind of need there, a need to get something from the visit, a sense of something lacking and of trying to get it from what was in the museum. And now I realised that that was simply not there any more. Not feeling a need for anything I did not experience a need to be there at all. It was fine to be there, but it would have been equally fine to have left. Since then, visiting museums is something that has simply not happened.

The greatest change of this kind, however, occurred in relation to painting and also aesthetics in general. As a child there was nothing I enjoyed more than drawing. I started painting seriously when I was twenty and for most of my adult life it has seemed like my vocation in life and, as such, I have always thought of myself as a painter. This sense of my identity being tied up with art came out most strongly in relation to aesthetics, and the sense of things, ordinary things in the world, being more or less aesthetically attractive. From the age of about sixteen onwards I became highly sensitised to the aesthetic qualities of things, how attractive or ugly they were. I would look at everything in these terms, from cutlery and crockery to buildings, interiors, clothes and shoes. Things that I found ugly used to cause me almost physical pain, while things that were aesthetically attractive – typically things from the past – I experienced as a kind of balm to the soul. This became so acute that it made life difficult, particularly in London where I always used to feel that there is so much ugliness. It was a significant part of the reason why I ended up moving to Paris, where in general most things are so much more aesthetically attractive. Through these years, I also tried to surround myself with things that were aesthetically attractive and to have as little as possible to do with ugly and functional things. Over time, this aversion to ugliness and the need for beauty weakened, but it was always there and right up to the retreat in Wales I continued to discriminate between everything according to how attractive or ugly they were.

This has all changed. It is not that I cannot see the ugliness or aesthetic attractiveness of things any more. It is all still there. But there is something else there, too, something far more fundamental and extraordinary that renders it irrelevant. When I look at anything now, even the most mundane or ordinary thing, it has a kind of wondrous quality. This quality is there in the litter in the street, or the dirt in the corner of the underground, as much as in the most exquisite Ming crockery or Regency furniture. 'As much as' is not quite right. It is the *same* quality. There is a uniformity to everything now, a uniformity of sheer wondrousness that makes whatever aesthetic qualities there are or are not seem unimportant. I can still see how much more elegant and refined is a Regency desk chair compared to the plastic, orange seats in the local café where I live, but in respect of this wondrous quality they are exactly the same and I find myself feeling the same reverent love for them both.

Alongside this, the desire to paint has collapsed. Apart from the week or two after my father told me that he was terminally ill with cancer, when I wanted to do nothing but paint, I have felt no urge to paint at all since coming back from Wales. When I think about it, this seems quite strange, but most of the time I do not think about it at all and it simply does not matter. Instead, it seems strange when people ask me how painting is going, or if they know that I have stopped and they ask me whether I have thought of starting again. It is as if something much, much deeper has shifted and with that shift the impulse to paint has simply gone. I do not know if I will ever paint again and it does not seem to matter one way or the other whether I do or not.

What became very rapidly apparent after the retreat in Wales was how much all these things, painting, the valuing of aesthetic attractiveness, museums and history, were all tied up with seeking. To a large extent, they all arose out of the held-sense of lack as something that I did to assuage it and so when that sense of lack fell away they did too.

Alongside the collapse of a sense of identification with aesthetic discrimination, painting, museums and history, there was also a general loss of identification with the values and opinions that I had held before. I come from a political family and grew up immersed in politics. Personally, I have never really believed that it is possible to make the world a 'better' place through political change, but despite this I have always held political opinions of various shades, often at the same time. After the trip to Wales, I found the conviction with which I held these opinions or values seemed largely to have evaporated. Instead of identifying with them personally, which is what I used to do, I find myself thinking of them conditionally. So, I no longer think that things are really right or wrong, but rather that if someone believes x then they will think y is right, whereas if they believe the opposite of x then they will think that z is right. What it amounts to, in a sense, is not really having any opinions about these things myself any more.

The reason why all these things happened, ultimately, is that what arose out of what happened in Wales was a much deeper realisation than I have ever felt before, even after Paris, that actually everything is one. This is why everything became home and is home. There is no longer a felt-sense of a real separation between things. Instead, it is clear that everything is really the same thing, just appearing as things that seem on the surface to be separate. The jug and the table-mat are not two things, but really only one thing somehow being both of them. Everything really is just oneness being that, as a kind of single, unified phenomenon. This single, unified phenomenon is simply 'what is'. This sense of 'what is', whatever it is, which opened up for the first time in Paris is there again now much more deeply and fully and it does not go. This 'what is' just *is*. It cannot be better or worse. Someone can prefer it to be one way or another, I can prefer it one way or another, but that does not mean that it really is 'better' like that. It is simply a personal preference, no more. All values or opinions, then, have become mere expressions of personal preference, conditional on those personal preferences. Ultimately, from an absolute perspective, there is no difference between any of them, just as there is no real difference between any of the outcomes they are opinions about.

Alongside the collapse of interest in history and museums, the absence of a desire to paint and the falling away of a sense of identification with certain values the other main change that was immediately evident after returning from the residential in Wales was the loss of a sense of identity in terms of my relationship to others, particularly my family. That I had had this sense of identity before is something that I only came to see in retrospect, now that it had altered. There had never been a time when I had not been a son or a brother. I had grown up in these relationships and they had formed part of my identity without my ever realising it. They were a part of my held-sense of who I was, so integral to that sense that I did not ever really notice them. And now, I realised, I did not feel defined in terms of them any more. This is not to say that I felt no connection to any member of my family, but rather that those connections no longer seemed to define me. In some sense, I was still my parents' son, but in another sense what I or 'this' was – because it felt clear that there is no real I – actually had nothing to do with them.

This distinction between 'I' and 'this' sums it up. The 'I' is the person Nigel Wentworth, who I took myself to be for so many years. That person was a white, English, man who painted, loved history and held certain political and non-political beliefs. He was also my parents' son, my sibling's brother. 'This' is none of those. It is not white, not English, not a man, does not paint, holds no views and has no relationship to anyone. There was no sense at the time of what 'this' was, only that it certainly did not have this identity. That identity was the constructed identity that the body-organism that is called 'Nigel Wentworth' had picked up over time. It had nothing to do with what 'this' was.

It was quite a disjointed feeling, in that I could sense that I no longer felt identified as Nigel Wentworth any more, but there was nothing positive in its place. The personal had collapsed to quite a significant extent to be replaced by an impersonal sense of being something, but what this 'something' was, was unclear to me. When I thought about it I could only describe myself as 'this', if I was honest, and not 'me' any more, but there was no sense of what 'this' was. By 'sense' I do not mean something intellectual, like an idea or belief, bur rather a lived-sense of being something; in the same way that my old sense of identity was not something that I believed about myself, but something that I carried around with me as much part of my make up as my body.

Another facet of the constructed identity of Nigel Wentworth that just seemed to disappear overnight was the sense of being defined by my past. Life by this stage had been a fairly long journey and I experienced myself before Wales as the person-at-that-stage-of-the-journey. That is to say, I experienced myself as being defined by all the things that had happened up to that point and by my projected sense of what might happen along the rest of the journey. I was the person to whom all of these things had happened in the past and to whom, possibly, these other things will happen in the future, up to my death. It was a kind of Janus-faced identity, looking back to the past and forward into the future.

Like most people, I had had a fairly chequered life, with quite a few ups and downs and more downs than ups to be honest. Some of the things that had happened I carried around with me as part of my identity. I was the person to whom 'this' had happened and 'that'. It was all part of who I was. All of this literally disappeared overnight. It is not that the events from my earlier life disappeared out of my memory. They did not. I could remember everything, just as before. But I no longer felt defined by them. All those things I could still remember, but they seemed to have happened to Nigel Wentworth and not to who, or what, I now experienced myself to be. Similarly, the sense of a projected future disappeared as well. Again, it is not that all sense of the future ended. It did not. There was still the knowledge that later in the day would come and tomorrow and next week and next year. But the sense that my identity was defined by what would happen during that time basically fell away.

This basic shift also manifested in relation to the cycle of becoming. Before going to the residential in Wales I had experienced myself as a 'person', called Nigel Wentworth, with a life that stretched back into the past and forward into the future. 'I' existed through a kind of endless movement from the past and into the future. This was the movement of becoming, that I had struggled with for so many years. I now saw that this had, as it were, a micro and a macro side to it. The micro side was the daily investment in a process of continual movement from 'here', which was experienced as lacking, to 'there' which I seemed to believe would be 'better'. The macro side was the sense of being a 'person' whose identity was defined by the nature and content of everything that had arisen out of the daily cycle of becoming. If that content in the past had been 'successful' then my identity was as a successful person. If it had been 'tragic' then my identity was as an unlucky person with a 'sad' life. By the same token, if the projected future was likely to be 'successful' or 'tragic', that would change my self-identity accordingly.

It was this sense of being a real 'person', with a real past and a real future that I realised had partially collapsed after the awakening in Wales. The effect of this was the loss of a sense of having any real identity, because this had only ever been constructed out of the remembered past and the projected future. Without the sense of being a real 'person' and without the sense of a held-identity there was nothing to ground a sense of myself as an entity subsisting through time and without that there could be no sense of there being an entity which was on a journey *to* anywhere. For, without a real entity continuing through time, how could there be any kind of journey? All that was left, then, was the experience of whatever seemed to be going on in the apparent moment. Whatever this is exists only in the timeless present. That is to say, without a sense of personal identity there is no continuity through time and so all that is left is whatever appears to be happening in the timeless present.

It is of the timeless present, rather than the present full stop, because the present only exists through the contrast with the past and the future and what became clear now was that there is no real past and no real future. Without a sense of myself as subsisting through time, my whole sense of time as real, and that is to say of the past and future as real, also began to collapse. All that is left is whatever seems to be happening. It became clear that the past only exists as another aspect of what appears only in the timeless present. The past is simply the present memories that I have about it and together these form the narratives that I tell myself, equally in the present, that make up 'the past' for me. It is the same with the future. The future is simply the imaginings and fantasies that I have about what might happen. Together these form the ever-shifting present narrative that I construct for myself. Just as my sense of my future changes as I move through life, so does my sense of my past. There is no such thing as *the* past, or *my* past. The past is a kaleidoscope made up of the more or less accurate memories and narratives that we hold to at present, according to our present perspective as to what is significant. Both the past and the future, then, are constructions out of thought. They have no substance beyond that.

The collapse of the sense of living from past to future is, therefore, at the same time and by the same movement, a collapse of the sense of living in a narrative. What appears to be happening is no longer experienced as a no narrative, or story. It does not come from anywhere and is not going anywhere. It just *is*.

One outcome of this is the gradual ending of becoming.

Becoming is the movement from past to future, typically to a 'better' future. Experiencing what is in the present as lacking because he feels separate from it, the 'person' projects a 'better' alternative or future and lives constantly in a movement towards that 'better' reality. With the collapse of the sense of being a real person there is both the end of the sense of being someone who subsists in time and also of there being any time to subsist in. So, there is no 'better' future for me to get to, because there is no future at all. There is only the timeless present and that has no direction to it. It has no past and no future. It just *is*. To live in the timeless present, then, is just to *be*, without any sense of becoming.

This does not mean that there is only a kind of dumb awareness of 'what is'. The brain carries on working and so thoughts continue to arise. There is still a sense of things happening, of being tired, or hungry or of needing to post a letter, or cook dinner. One still carries on doing things and engaging in the world. There is not a collapse into complete passivity or aimlessness. Also, there are still thoughts about what is going on over a longer term, for instance, what happened a few months ago and what might happen next year. These kinds of narratives still arise, but the energy gradually goes out of them, because the sense of there being someone here, a 'person' to whom they are really happening, has largely gone.

What does it mean to say 'the energy goes out of them'? Before, there was an investment in the narratives that were told because they were held to describe reality, my reality. Before there was a sense of being a real person, with a real life, to whom real things happened that had a real significance. Now, nothing seems more fanciful and unreal. With the seeing through of that reality, the seeing of it as a dreamed reality, the investment in it seeps away. The content of the narratives is now seen to have nothing to do with what I really am. The thoughts or narratives are only something transient that happen to arise, or not as the case may be. They are not me. All there is is whatever appears to be arising. The narratives are simply another thing that seem to appear.

With the winding down of becoming, the winding down of the

movement towards a 'better' place somewhere in an imagined future, all that comes to be left is being. Being does not come from anywhere and is not going anywhere. It just *is*. For the first time in many, many years I found that I just *was* and it felt entirely natural, as if I had come back to what I had always really been. And I now realise that something in me had always had a sense of this. It was because of this that I had always felt that the identity that was Nigel Wentworth was not what I really was. Something in me had always known it. After coming back from the retreat in Wales it began to be not just known, but also lived.

The end of becoming is the end of movement from 'here' to somewhere else, somewhere 'better'. It comes with the collapse of the sense of separation that makes 'here' seem lacking. Without that sense of lack, 'here' has nothing wrong with it. It becomes home. This is why after the retreat, there was an overwhelming sense of having come home and of being at home. Everything felt like home and I realised that it always had been home, only I had not been able to see it. I had always been trying to get there and it was precisely 'me' being there trying to get to this 'better' place that I imagined home to be, that prevented 'what is', which is all there ever had been, from feeling like home. At first, I worried that it might go, that I might go back to feeling not at home. It was the realisation that I always had been at home that made me see that it would not go. The sense of home was not some kind of special state, some temporary experience brought on by something that I had done, that would end just as it had started. Home was simply being where I had always been only now it felt completely different to how it had always been experienced in that nothing seemed to be lacking any more.

The fact that it was very ordinary made complete sense to me. I had always distrusted the whole idea of 'special states of consciousness' that are sometimes talked about in the world of contemporary spirituality and had never been interested in pursuing anything like that. All I had ever wanted was to be able to *be*, in the way that a tree was, and not just trees. Everything else in the world, apart from human beings, just *was*, fence panels, lemons, tables, cats, the dirt in the underground. It was only people who seemed to be unable to do this most simple of things. So, it had always been clear to me that what was lacking was not some kind of special state of consciousness that had to be attained, something higher or better than where we already are, but rather that it was our natural inherence that had somehow been lost. And now something had shifted and it became obvious that I always had been at home, only I had not been able to see it.

The way of being that arises from the experience of being back at home is sometimes described as being like the flow that artists and extreme sports people experience. To me, however, it seems very different. It is true that there is a temporary suspension of the sense of being a subject in flow, but it is only temporary and it is still a person who paints or sky dives, only they are lost, or absorbed, in the activity they are doing. The sense of home for me is quite different. It is the opposite of being lost or absorbed. There is a sense of being present, but not as a 'person' and without the sense of being separate from anything. Everything appears perfect just as it is and there is no sense of things needing to be different from how they are. There is, therefore, no movement away from what is and so the spur to action is absent. Being home also brings a sense of wonder, as even the simplest thing is seen to be a miracle when it is seen as something that has never been seen before. This sense of wonder interestingly seems to reduce the more there is a movement into practical activity that is goal-oriented, and it returns when that slows down again. It is because of this that there is an increasing loss of interest in doing very much. 'Doing' nothing, as it were, seems to arise more and more.

The sense of being real, a real 'person', then, brings with it a sense of being separate and of everything being apart from each other. Without the sense of being a person there is no sense of real separation. Instead, everything seems whole or complete. The falling away of the sense of being a separate person is then, at the same time, the falling into wholeness. Wholeness is always actually the reality, it is just that 'I' cannot see it, because 'I' – the person who experiences himself or herself to be real – feels separate from everything.

The sense of wholeness is also one of fullness, in which it is realised that nothing is missing and therefore nothing is needed. For me, at first, this sense of fullness felt like being full to bursting. The nearest thing I could describe it as being like would be being in love. Later, it became softer or quieter; a simple sense of nothing being lacking. As many teachers of non-duality say, this is our natural state. It is only the experience of personal reality that brings a sense of lack and of something being missing and therefore needed.

The emotional dimension of this sense of fullness and of nothing being lacking was the presence of massive joy. Over time, like the rest of what arose after awakening, it has gradually quietened down, becoming a simple, natural sense of well-being. Here joy bubbles up like warm water out of a spring. Again, this is natural. When a person feels joy typically they attribute it to the object that brought it on. For example, if a person is trying to buy a house and after a long time it finally goes through, they might experience a short period of joy. Typically, they will attribute this joy to that fact that the house purchase has at last gone through. Actually, it is the other way round. Joy is the natural state for man, arising out of a natural sense of wholeness. All that happens for the person who experiences themselves as separate is that when something goes well, like the house purchase, it temporarily removes the sense of lack that they carry within themselves because they feel real and therefore separate. This returns them to their natural state, which is one of wholeness or fullness, in which their natural joy arises. Unfortunately, however, the sense of wholeness or fullness does not last, as the sense of lack that results from the held-sense of personal reality inevitably returns. This brings in its train a return of the feeling of dissatisfaction and the pursuit of a new object to bring back a sense of wholeness and joy, now the effect of the house purchase has worn off. And so the cycle continues, endlessly. In the absence, therefore, of an inherent sense of lack, as arises through the experience of personal reality and so separation, there is only a sense of completeness or wholeness and therefore of natural joy.

As well as feeling a bursting sense of joy after coming back from

Wales, I also found myself feeling a love for everybody in a way that I have never felt before. This started in Wales, where I found myself wanting to hug everyone on the retreat. But it carried on once I got home and I found myself wanting to hug everybody in the street or on the tube. It had nothing to do with liking them as a person or caring about their story. So far from wanting to help them make their story work as well as possible, the problem seemed the story itself, born out of the sense of personal reality that they carried with them. What I felt was rather a kind of love for them in their beingness and had nothing to do with their particular identity as a 'person'.

The love was not just in me, but in everything else too. There was a sense of everything as being pure love, the glass of water on the table, the sound of the fridge motor, the sunlight shining on the houses opposite. I cannot describe what this was like, but it was the most wondrous feeling.

The last thing that came in the immediate aftermath of the Wales retreat was a deepening of the realisation that seeking really was over for me. Having come home there was simply nothing to seek for. It was clear that I had found, as it were, what I had been seeking for thirty five years, only 'I' had not found it. With everything feeling whole and full there was no sense of anything being lacking and therefore nothing that needed finding. The collapse of the seeking energy and the drive it fuelled in life was like the puncturing of a balloon. All the tautness and tension went out of it and there was the sense of a massive relaxation. There was no drive to do anything very much really. This was not a problem because everything felt whole and complete just as it was. But it felt quite odd, so used was I to living in that way; always on the move from one thing onto the next, always searching, always seeking.

How complete this end of seeking was became apparent at the next meeting of Tony's, which was a week after I got back from Wales. I went along expecting it to be the same as all the others and instead it was completely different. For the previous few years, since I had started going, I had heard Tony talk about all this and it was as if he was standing on the other side of a screen describing something that I could not see. I would strain to understand, but simply could not really get it. Now, in this first meeting after the retreat as he spoke, it was as if I was standing on the other side of the screen with him looking at what he was talking about. Repeatedly I found myself saying to myself, 'oh that is what you mean by x'. It was a strange experience, wonderful and funny at the same time.

I have continued going to the meetings, but the sense I had before of going there in order to try to get something is absent. And when I speak with other people and they talk of wanting to go to listen to this or that person I realise that all of that is over for me now.

What Does it Mean to Wake Up?

There are countless ways in which a 'person' can try to make their experience 'better'. They can do all sorts of therapies to learn to understand themselves better and why they are the way they are. They can do different forms of exercise that will make them fitter, healthier, stronger and supposedly more attractive. They can do spiritual exercises, like prayer, or meditation or mindfulness to become calmer, more centred or more compassionate. All of them are aimed at making the outcome for the 'person' in the flow of their life more pleasant or satisfying. There is nothing wrong with any of this, but it is completely different from awakening. Awakening is not about the outcomes for the person in the flow of their life becoming 'better', rather it is the end of the sense of there being a real person who has a life at all in the first place.

Awakening is waking up to the impersonal reality that there are no people, not oneself nor anyone else. So nothing is really happening to anyone because there is no one for anything to happen to. Everything that happens does so impersonally, by no one and for no one.

Therefore, it is not the person who wakes up. Rather, there is the waking up *from* the delusion of being a real person and from the sense that there ever had been such a person.

It is hard to over-emphasise this point. The whole of ordinary human life, really the *whole* of it, is about us trying to make things better for ourselves. Everything that we do, our work, our leisure, our relationships and friendships are about trying to make our experience as good as possible. And the structures of society reflect that. Our political systems, judicial systems, educational systems, health systems, the whole of our scientific establishment, have at their root the aim of trying to make the experience of 'people' as good as possible. All of it rests on the twin assumptions that there are real people in the world and that it is possible to make their experience, the outcomes in the flow of their lives, better. One effect of awakening is seeing through both of these as mere delusions.

Describing awakening as the seeing-through of the delusion of being a 'person' makes it sound cognitive, like an intellectual awareness or perception. Nothing could be further from the truth. No amount of intellectual understanding of the theory of non-duality – the view that everything is ultimately one[3] – will ever amount to awakening. It would be possible for a 'person' to understand everything within non-duality intellectually, the nature and pointlessness of seeking, the illusion of separation, that a 'person' is a construction through conditioning and so on, without anything changing at all. Awakening is not a 'person' coming to understand something, rather it is a shift on a deep level within the body-organism such that there is an opening to the nature of ultimate reality. This was clearly what happened sitting on the floor in Paris. In Wales, because what happened occurred during the night when I was asleep, I do not know what it was, but it is clear from the effect that it has had over a long time what must have happened. It is as if there is a temporary letting go of the whole held-sense of being a person and consequently an opening out to a reality that is immeasurable and boundless. To adapt a metaphor from Plato;

---

[3]Non-duality is a modern Western term. The tradition behind it is Advaita Vedanta, a branch of Hinduism.

human beings are like creatures who live their lives out in caves in which there is only very limited light. As a result everything appears different from how it actually is and strange shadows are cast upon the walls of the cave as they move about. Because this is all they have ever known and they cannot see how things actually are, they believe everything they see and experience, including the shadows on the wall, to be real. Awakening is like a bright light being turned on within the cave making everything visible for what it really is. The light does not generally stay on, however, at least not at that intensity, but goes back out again, at least to some extent. Afterwards, however, even though the same shadows can be seen on the wall they no longer look real but are seen to be mere shadows thrown up by things moving around. The thrall that the appearance of things had before on the people simply goes. Everything still seems the same in one way, but in another it is clear that it is all utterly different.

Practically, then, awakening is the seeing through of the delusions that form the experience of a 'person', though metaphysically it is something much, much deeper. These delusions are based ultimately upon the held-sense that I am a person, a real person who also has free will and choice and so can act in the world to try to make my experience as good as possible. Because I experience myself as a real person, so I also experience all the other people as real and everything else in the world as real too. The world is a real world, full of real objects and I can interact with them, using the free will that I have, to try to make things go as well as possible for myself. That is the dream that human beings live in. Awakening is the seeing through of that dream.

It is important to state that awakening is only the seeing through of the sense of being a person; it is typically not the end of that sense. When awakening happens there is not the instantaneous collapse of everything that makes up the 'person'. The 'person' as well as being constituted by a held-sense of personal reality is also a construct that results from the conditioning that has gone on for the whole of that body organism's life. That conditioning is still there, it does not just vanish. So, the body-organism can continue to behave very much as it did before. What is no longer there in the same way, however, is the underlying held-sense that this is what one really is. It is seen that the 'person' one took oneself to be before is just a construct of the conditioning and that what one really is, as it were, is something completely 'other'. I say that one realises that it is only 'as it were' that one is something completely 'other' because the whole point is the loss of the sense of being a real person. So, it is not I who it is realised is something 'other', for precisely what is realised is that there is no real I in the first place to be anything at all, 'other' or not.

The fact that typically in awakening there is not the collapse of the whole sense of being a person means that aspects of the conditioning of the 'person', like opinions, or values, can survive. They are just not identified with any more in the way that they were before. So, for example, I might still shake my head in disbelief and a certain sadness when I read that some American politicians continue to describe all the evidence of global warming as 'just weather'. But that does not mean that I believe that the opinion that global warming is ultimately real and that it would be a good idea to try to do something to stop it is really 'mine', or defines 'me', or that it is even really true. It is simply that the holding of these opinions is part of the effect of past conditioning 'here', and that in albeit a weakened form it continues to exist. Alongside it there is now another perception, that there is only 'what is', or appears to be, as the expression of oneness, including the phenomenon we call 'global warming'. Whether global warming continues to occur or not does not change the underlying reality that everything is one. Nothing does. And therefore, it does not ultimately matter. The idea that it does is really just another part of the dream.

Another facet of the sense of being a 'person' is the having of a persona; the way by which the self presents itself to what it experiences as the world. The seeing through of the sense of being a person is also the seeing through of the persona as well, for if there is not really anybody there, there is nobody to present to the world. All that is left is the sense of being 'this', a body-organism that happens to have a certain make up and to have received a certain conditioning. This body-organism does not try to present itself in a particular way, because it no longer has a felt-need for things from other people and so no longer feels pressed to try to behave in the ways it believes will ensure other people will behave towards it as it need them to. The result will be a more or less gradual collapse of the persona to be replaced by a natural straightforwardness, one that will vary in style from person to person.

This straightforwardness also comes with the end of a sense of specialness. Part of what results from the sense of lack, that itself results from the sense of being real and so apart, is a desire for specialness, that is to be special oneself, for one's experiences to be special or to get to a 'better' or more special place. Spiritual enlightenment is often seen as the ultimate special place to get to, where someone becomes saintly, or all loving. This delusion of specialness is another thing that is seen through in awakening. It goes because with the seeing through of the delusions of personal reality and identity it is equally seen that there is nothing apart to be more special than anything else. This loss of the need to be special can appear as a form of humility. Humility is generally understood as a 'personal' attribute, as a person being humble. This is not that. It is not the expression of a 'person' who does not feel themselves to be special, it is the absence of the sense of really being someone at all, which then naturally presents itself as what would be experienced as humility. It is not so much personal humility in reality, however, as the expression of a sense of personal nothingness.

As well as the seeing through of the sense of being a person, and therefore of personal separation from everything else that appears to be, awakening is at the same time, by the same movement, the seeing through of the sense of separation and separateness in general. If 'what is' is an undifferentiated wholeness such that there is no 'I' separate from what appears as the table and the jug, then nor are the table and the jug separate from each other. Really, there is no separation anywhere. This is what comes to be seen through awakening and it is the most profound shift that takes place. Again, it is not instantaneous. It is not that one day there is a sense of being a separate person and that everything is separate from everything else, and the next day there is just a uniform sense of 'what is' as an undifferentiated expression of oneness. It is not like that. The held-sense of being separate is the deepest facet of what makes up a 'person'. It is seen through in awakening, for that is precisely how awakening manifests, but that does not mean that it goes completely or instantly.

That the sense of separateness does not go completely comes in part from the fact that we continue to live in the phenomenal, or relative, world. This phenomenal world is the expression of oneness, but it does not appear as that. Rather it appears as multiplicity. It is full of apparently separate things; tables, jugs, cats, pear trees, fridge motor whirring sounds and sensations of cold to list but a few. In ordinary experience these things appear separate or apart from each other and something of this experience of apartness survives awakening. A jug is still seen as being in a way apart from the table it sits on, otherwise we would have no thought to pick it up off the table and pour the water out of it. But it is only seen 'in part' in this way, because precisely what goes in awakening is the sense that this apparent apartness is real. So, the jug continues to be seen as apart from the table in one sense, though in another it is no longer seen as really separate or apart at all. What results from this is an ambiguous perception or experience, in which things seem both apart and not apart at the same time. This is another way of saying that everything is seen as oneness somehow appearing as lots of separate things.

From the fact that what goes in awakening is the sense of being a real person what also goes at the same time and by the same movement is any sense of awakening as some kind of special state that can be attained, or as being special in any way at all. This idea is itself only in fact an expression of a dualistic perspective. For, if to be awakened is to be in a special state then not to be awakened would mean to be in a different or worse place, and this idea that there are different places some of which are more special, or better, than others is pure dualism. This idea also comes from the belief that somehow awakening is something that happens to a 'person'[4]. At the

---

[4]The inverted commas here are to make clear that it is the fictional entity
    that takes itself to be real that is being referred to.

core of what makes up a 'person' is the whole structure of becoming, the endless movement to a 'better' place. The belief that awakening is some kind of special state is the incorporation of awakening into the world-view of a 'person', its reduction down to just another 'better' place that the 'person' can get to.

This has radical consequences for the seeker. The seeker experiences himself as separate and therefore has a sense of something lacking that needs to be made good. Awakening is often seen as the ultimate solution to this perceived problem, the achievement of a state in which the pain and suffering of ordinary human life is absent. And it is typically for this reason that the seeker seeks awakening. Anything the seeker seeks, however, can only be another thing that he tries to get for himself, another expression of the energy of becoming born out of the sense of personal reality and so separation. Therefore, it can never give the seeker what the seeker craves, which is an end to the very suffering of separation. Moreover, because seeking is precisely the expression of the energy of 'personal' becoming born out of the sense of 'personal' being, the more the seeker seeks awakening the more he reinforces the very sense of 'personal' being and so separation that is the perceived problem in the first place. Seeking then is not just futile but self-defeating.

This again is hard to overstate. The conviction the seeker has is that he can get to this 'better' place that he craves and that he can get there by seeking, that is by trying things, doing things, making an effort. The more the seeker does this, however, the more he reinforces the held-sense that he really is a person with free will and choice who can really make things 'better' for himself by choosing to do 'this' or not do 'that'. But it is precisely this held-sense of being a real person that keeps the seeker from seeing that he does not need to get anywhere else, to any 'better' place, because where he is is already home and always was. It is the ultimate paradox. It is seeking that sustains the sense of being separate for the seeker. So, the more the seeker seeks the more entrenched he will become in his experience of himself as being really separate and so of needing to seek in order to get to a 'better' place where the experience of separation is absent. And so it goes on and on and on.

I had experienced this from the sharp end many years earlier from my teens onwards when I found self-seeking unbearable, but also that anything that I did to try to stop self-seeking was only in fact another expression of self-seeking, thereby reinforcing my suffering. I now found myself looking at exactly the same paradox, but from the other side of the wall as it were. It looks so straightforward from here, but I know from bitter personal experience how awful it can feel on the other side. From here, though, as well as seeming quite tragic, it can also appear terribly comical; people who are already at home trying to get there and this very attempt to get there making them feel that they are not in fact there already! Perhaps this is what I was laughing at so much when I woke up that morning in Wales.

What this means is that the whole of seeking is not just futile and self-defeating, but also completely unnecessary. The sense of separation only ever is a delusion. Nothing really is separate from anything else. There is nothing else, nowhere else, and so nowhere 'better' to get to. All the seeker ever wanted already is, as everything that ever is or has ever happened. There is nothing that is not that. The chair that you are sitting on is that, the sitting on it is that, the sounds you can hear are that and so are the sensations that you feel, the perceptions you see and the thoughts that pass through your head. Everything that ever is and everything that ever happens to 'you' is that. So, it is not just that there is nowhere better to get to, but there never was any need for any effort to get there. For everything that is ever wanted is already here.

The other facet of awakening that makes it clear that it is not something that happens to a person, not something that the person gains, or acquires, is that it is precisely the sense of being a real person that is lost. Awakening manifests as the seeing through of the sense of being a real, separate person. With that comes the loss of some, or all, of what constituted the 'person' before. For me, that was the falling away of the motivation to paint that had been the mainstay of my life for thirty years, the loss of various interests, such as in history and museums, the collapse of an identification with the values of aesthetic quality and the weakening of the sense of being defined by my relationships. For someone else, it will be other things, perhaps more, perhaps less. What it will not be, however, is the gaining of anything. There will *only* be loss.

This is entirely natural and obvious, though the seeker cannot see it. The seeker only knows trying to get things for himself, after all, that is what seeking is. All the seeker can do, all the seeker ever does do, is seek. So, the seeker imagines that he will gain something through awakening, in the same way as he believes he can gain something though all the other things that he does, or that happen to him. Awakening, however, is not something that happens to a 'person'. It is rather the seeing through of the sense of being a real person in the first place. Inevitably, what comes with that is the loss of some of what had constituted the 'person' who had been there previously. Some of the identity of that 'person' will go.

And it is only by that happening, by the collapse of some at least of what previously constituted the identity of the 'person', that the realisation can arise that there is only in fact oneness, only in fact wholeness without any separation. The identity is the concrete form of the held-sense of personal being. To the extent that it is there the sense of personal being and with it separation is there and therefore the absence of a sense of wholeness. The one has to go for the other to be.

Why Does Awakening Occur?

This reality of what awakening is has consequences for an understanding of how awakening occurs. The seeker believes that he is a separate person with free will and choice. Precisely what comes to be seen through awakening is that there never was such a person. Therefore, nobody chose to do something, or was responsible for doing something, that made awakening happen. More fundamentally, nobody actually woke up. What happened was that the apparent body organism, as it were, woke up from the delusion of being a real and therefore separate person, or being separate at all. It is the sense of personal being or personal reality that falls away and it is this at root that constitutes the 'person'.

Therefore, awakening does not occur because of anything that a 'person' thought they did or experienced themselves as doing. This is a real problem for the seeker, because the seeker lives in becoming, in wanting and trying to get to a 'better' place and knows nothing else. The seeker therefore does not want to hear this and in a sense cannot hear it. What the seeker wants to hear is that there is a 'better' place to get to and that he can get there if only he will do the right things, for instance, pray devoutly enough, or meditate for long enough, or eat the right foods, or be 'good' enough. It is this need that the world's religions and spiritual teachings feed with their ubiquitous lists of things that the seeker needs to do in order to get to wherever it is they want to get to, be it heaven, nirvana, enlightenment, paradise or wherever.

The seeker cannot hear this because the seeker is caught up in the thrall and apparent drama of being a real person in a real world, which arises from the held-sense of personal being. This held-sense is not just a belief. If it was it could be dispelled by just not believing it. And that can easily be seen not to work. The sense of personal being is a *held*-sense, which is to say that it is part of the lived-reality for the organism, part of the very fabric of its being, of its very make up, that it carries around with it. As such, everything is experienced *in terms of* this sense of personal reality. Everything that happens is experienced as happening *to* 'me' or that 'I' am actually doing it. Because of this held-sense of personal reality and the way it colours the whole of the seeker's experience, the seeker cannot but believe that he can act to make his experience 'better' and simply cannot see that that is a delusion.

But if awakening does not occur because of anything that the seeker did then how does it occur? The short answer is that it just happens at least apparently. Obviously, if there are no separate people with free will and choice and so if there is nobody who is actually doing anything, then that is the only way it could occur, because everything actually occurs that way. Nobody really does anything and nobody ever really did do anything. It all just happens. The longer answer is in the form of a different 'story' of the apparent process in each case. It is only a story or narrative, however, because if there are no really separate people then nothing is really happening to anybody at all.

The 'story' here runs something like this. When I first came across Tony's message most of it chimed with my previous experience on the basis of what had happened in Paris, that the seeming separation we experience is an illusion, that it is all an expression or instantiation of an underlying unity or oneness and that the self-seeking that constitutes life for the 'person' is futile. There was a wonderful sense of finding someone who was singing from the same hymn sheet. For so many years I had experienced things a certain way but never found anybody else who seemed to do so. Therefore, going to his meetings and hearing him speak felt like a kind of homecoming. There were things he said, however, that were new to me and, generally, what I found was that at each meeting he would say something that seemed to go straight through me. For the rest of the meeting I would be lost in a kind of reverie and could not really concentrate on what was being said. It was as if something in what he said struck a chord within me and the whole of my being became filled with it. Tony describes this as resonance. Resonance is not intellectual understanding. When something resonates it is completely different from 'getting' something intellectual, like understanding something in a classroom or lecture theatre. It is as if something within us vibrates to the words that we hear. How is that possible? Ultimately, there are no separate people, just as there are no separate cats or trees or stones. And something in us knows this. The 'person', the seeker, cannot hear the message of non-duality and cannot understand it. But something else does. Something else knows that we are not really this personal identity we pretend to be. This 'something else' hears the words that are spoken to it and resonates with them.

Over a longer period of time, what I came to notice was that there seemed to be a kind of shifting of things going on. I did not understand what it was, or what it meant, but over time it was clear that something was, as it were, falling into place. I came to see it as a kind of kaleidoscope that was gradually turning and that as it did everything was reorganising itself into a new form bit by bit, bit by bit. This process started as a kind of intellectual clarity and gradually became something deeper, something more lived. But it was only ever somewhat more lived, it was never really lived before the trip to Wales. I used to hear Tony talk about things, for instance, describing the wall as 'oneness walling' and I would look at the wall and wonder what he meant. Because of the minor awakening that had happened in Paris I knew what he was saying was true. But I could not really see it. This carried on right up to the weekend in Pax Lodge, where a much deeper shift seemed to occur, which seemed to begin the process that culminated in what happened in Wales.

All of this is a story. For each of the awakenings that have happened a story could be told. In Paris, it was to do with reaching a place of despair after so many years of running away from the anguish I felt within. In Pax Lodge it was to do with a letting go to not knowing after decades of holding on to needing to 'know' the answer to life. And in Wales it was the culmination of the whole process of seeing through the sense of being a 'person. But each of these is just a story.

What I mean by that is not just that 'I' did not do these things, but that they did not really happen at all. It is not that 'I' did not let go to unknowing in Pax Lodge, in the sense of 'I' as a separate person with free will and choice deciding to do that. It is that in a sense, it did not really happen to me at all. The idea that this happened to me, but that 'I' did not make it happen, is still the expression of the idea that though there are no people with free will and choice, there still are real people. According to this idea, though no one really does anything, or chooses to do anything and everything just happens these things that happen are real. So, I am not choosing to type these words, it is just happening; but it is still really happening. In the same way, I did not choose to let go to unknowing at Pax Lodge, but it did really happen. That is still to be caught up in the thrall of the experience of a 'person' for whom everything is real. What is seen in awakening is precisely that it is not. It is not that I am just not choosing to type these words it is that it is not really happening at all. Similarly, it is not that you are not choosing to read them, reading them is not really happening at all. Instead, there is only oneness, manifesting as everything that appears to be. So, my typing these words is just oneness manifesting as that and so is you reading them. The letting go to unknowing that happened at Pax Lodge, then, was just oneness manifesting as that. It was not something that happened to me, as the story would have it, at all.

Another way of seeing this is in terms of 'stopping' and 'letting go', and what each of these is. Each of the awakenings can be understood as a kind of stopping and letting go. In Paris there was the stopping of running away from the anguish and a kind of letting go to it whatever that might mean. At Pax Lodge there was the stopping of needing to know and a letting go to unknowing. And this led to the much greater stopping and letting go that happened in Wales. Perhaps this is why there is an emphasis on 'stopping' within the world of non-duality. Many teachers, from different traditions, speak of the need to 'stop'.

But a 'person' cannot stop. To be a 'person' is to be in an endless movement of becoming. It is not so much that that is what a 'person' is in, as that is what a 'person' is; a 'person' is becoming. So, a 'person' cannot stop. Stopping and letting go, then, are things that can only ever arise as something that just happens. So, does stopping and letting go cause awakening? No. This is again just a story, a story the 'person' would like to believe, for then he would only have to find a way to stop and let go and he would wake up.

The stopping and letting go that happened in Paris occurred only because of *everything* that had happened before, all the hundreds of times when I had turned away from the anguish and sought a way to escape it through distraction or whatever. And each of those events had occurred because of what had occurred before them, and so on and so on. No single event causes another event but is in fact tied to all the others. They all form a unified whole, like a tapestry, in which each stitch, whilst appearing separate, is actually tied into all the others. The stopping and letting go no more caused the awakening than any other event in my life, for instance catching the bus when I was nineteen on the way back from work, for they all form a unified whole. A person's apparent life, then, forms a single movement, or whole, made up equally of everything that happens along the way. No single part of it causes another, for it is all one.

Permanent and Temporary/Delayed Awakenings

Awakening, I have said, is the seeing through of the sense of being a person, but it is not the end of that sense. That is typically how it is for most human beings. There are some body organisms, however, for whom it is all over in an instant, apparently. I have never met anyone like this, but I have heard that they exist. For most human beings, however, the sense of a person comes back again at some point after awakening. And that was how it was for me. After I came back from Wales there was a sense of being home again, after many, many years of estrangement. Alongside that, there was the collapse of certain features of what had been my identity before, seeing myself as a painter, the interest in history and museums and so on. Other facets of my identity did not go, however, for instance, seeing myself as a parent, as English and a man. It was not so much that these things 'came back' at some point later, but rather that they never went. It was as if an earthquake had occurred beneath the foundations to a house and half of it had just collapsed. The other half, however, had remained standing, albeit a lot less stable and securely grounded than it had been before.

Another metaphor that is sometimes used is that of an aperture in a camera. Awakening is like the complete opening of the aperture, letting in vast amounts of light. Usually, the aperture then shuts back closed again, though it never goes back to its original position. Some degree of openness to the light remains permanently. This had happened to me after Paris, after which there remained a permanent sense that everything really is one and the anguish that had plagued my life for eight years never returned. But it was much more true after the retreat in Wales. It is hard to describe how fundamental a shift this was, despite everything that remained. It was like going from a place where on a basic level I felt myself to be a 'person', though knowing somewhere that that was not really true, to another place in which there was no real sense of being a person at all, though quite a lot of what had previously felt like me was strangely still there.

What resulted from this can best be described as a schizophrenic existence; one in which there was the living of two quite different modes of being alongside each other. Most of the time, particularly when I was alone, there would be just the living of everything as the expression of oneness, wondrous and still. Out of this would arise a joy and sense of well-being, that often was quite blissful. And then other situations would arise, jobs I had to do, dealings with people and so much of what I had to do as a parent and suddenly Nigel Wentworth would be back, with all the familiar roles, attitudes, values and ways of expressing myself. It was really quite disconcerting, like being two people, or living out two existences at the same time, only in one body.

This was not completely black and white, however, though at the time the difference did seem quite stark. It was like being a machine that had always been working, whirring and clunking away, and now out of the blue had started idling a lot of the time. Suddenly the machine would start up again and all the motors and cogs and gears would be going like the clappers and then just as suddenly it would fall silent again and there would be an ethereal sense of quiet where previously there had been so much noise. There was no set rhyme or reason to when the machine came back on and when it fell silent, though there was something of a pattern to it, in that when I was engaged with other people 'I' was much more likely to be there, whereas when I was on my own it was not. But it was not black and white. Some of the time, when I was walking along the road by myself, for instance, 'I' would be walking along and sometimes there would just be walking along happening without a sense that 'I' was there.

The way this to-ing and fro-ing manifests between experiencing myself as a 'person' and not is something like as follows: during the times when there is only what appears to be happening the idea that life is a personal drama seems like a fairy story. The investment that we as 'people' have in that story then seems ridiculous. The idea that anything is really happening at all in the way that it appears to be or that it has any real significance seems absurd. Everything clearly is just a wondrous impersonal manifestation going nowhere. But then something shifts and the sense that 'I' am there is back again. Things now seem not only to be really happening, but to be happening *to* 'me'. With that, the sense that there is a real drama going on again returns and with it the sense that I am obviously the lead actor in it. Things that go 'wrong' in the drama are taken personally, causing 'me' to suffer and so the whole struggle with life, to try to bend reality to make it as 'I' need it to be, starts up again.

The words 'I' and 'me' are in inverted commas because they do not stand for anything. There is no thing that is I or me. These are just words that we use to stand for what in the dream world we experience as an object, the self. But actually there is nothing there that they refer to. The self is just a delusional held-sense. Therefore, it is not the case that before awakening I did things, but now I do not any more. Nor is it the case that when the sense of a 'person' returns that I am back doing things, but when it is absent everything just happens. There never was a real person that was me and so I never do anything and never have done. When we experience ourselves as real people we are simply caught up in a delusional dream state in which agency and responsibility are attributed where actually there is none. So no one ever did anything and therefore no one is responsible for anything. It all just happens.

The philosopher David Hume described the attributing of meaning and value to features of the world as the 'gilding and staining' of the world. What he meant was that everything that occurs in the world is actually normatively neutral, that is without intrinsic meaning or value. It just is. Nothing is really beautiful or ugly, good or bad. These are not qualities that actually occur in the world. Rather, they are projected onto the world by people. The root of this projection of normativity onto the world is the sense that everything that occurs within my experience is not just happening but is happening to a person, to 'me'. On the basis of this underlying personalised experience, those things that I like I come to see as 'good' and those things that I do not like I come to see as 'bad'. Most other 'people' experience these things in a similar way, giving rise to a socially grounded morality, or set of rules, laying out which actions are proscribed and which are condoned or even praised. On the foundation of this underlying set of rules the superstructures that are the legal, judicial and penal systems are then created.

If, after awakening, there is return of the sense of being a 'person', and consequently a somewhat schizophrenic existence of experiencing oneself some of the time as being there as a real person and some of the time not, this typically occurs alongside a gradual deepening of what was realised through awakening and with that an equally gradual weakening and crumbling of the structures of what had previously constituted that 'person's' sense of identity. It is as if once the aperture has opened to a certain point, even though it might close back up considerably afterwards, though never to where it was before, there is a natural movement back towards the fuller opening that occurred originally. Over time, then, the sense of being a real person comes back less and less often and also less strongly when it does return. There is a gradual shift towards the constant absence of a sense of personal being and so of a personal drama going on.

This raises the question of whether there is a final state that awakening tends towards of complete depersonalisation. Given how recently all this happened 'here' I am not in a position to comment too much on this. Even in the moments that are most impersonal 'here', there is still the sense when hunger arises, for instance, that it is my hunger and not the chair's. Some sense of a centre clearly remains, and other human beings who have woken up say the same thing. Even someone as sage-like as Nisargadatta[5], in response to a question about this, acknowledged that so long as there is the body some of the characteristics of the person survive. And even Jesus in the garden of Gethsemane was torn between a 'personal' agenda, which was to flee, and his awakened sense that what was happening was the will of God and that to give in to the 'personal' impulse to run away would be to deny everything that he knew to be true. The conditioning that forms the character, therefore, does not just go after awakening and however much that conditioning might crumble over time, it seems that some features of the 'person' remain.

I have said that awakening was the seeing through of the sense of being a real, separate person. With that came the collapse of some of what made up that character, though other aspects of the constructed identity remained. Then, over time, a gradual crumbling of what remains typically takes place and that is what has happened 'here'. The other side of this is the gradual loss of the whole sense of being a person at all. This is hard to describe, but over time it becomes one of the most obvious features of what makes up the shift that is called awakening.

Before, there was a held-sense of being a person, a real person. I was here, I really did things, things really happened to me. I had a life, which had started a long time ago and during which all sorts of things had happened, which had made me who I was today. And, I hoped, my life would continue long into the future up to my death. And I would really die. That was another thing that would really happen. All of this was not just something that I thought or believed; I felt it in my bones. This is what I mean by saying that it was a held-sense, for it was something that I felt and carried around within my body as my whole sense of myself. So far from being a thought or belief itself, it was what grounded and informed every thought and every belief I had. So, when I thought about needing to do some shopping, that was something that 'I' was going to do, this real person who was here. Equally, if I thought about a conversation that I had at

---

[5]Nisargadatta Maharaj. 1897-1981. One of the great teachers of Advaita in Twentieth Century India

work yesterday, again that was something that really happened to 'me'. The same for any thought about anything in the future, that was something that would really happen to 'me', or that 'I' would do.

It is hard to overstate the significance in the life of a human being of this held-sense of being a real person. It is the glue that holds it all together, the ground of the meaning that all of it seems to have, the fuel that provides the energy that drives it all. It creates a sense of a centre, 'me', that is experienced as being like the main actor in a dramatic play. Everything seems very real, full on and meaningful, to 'me'. But it also somewhere feels fundamentally lacking, as if something has been lost. Often this is so subtle and felt so deeply that it is not really noticed. And yet it gives rise to the endless agitation, movement and becoming that characterises human life.

It is this whole held-sense of being a real person that gradually weakens after awakening, like the gradual going out of a candle. It is quite undramatic. Most of the time, nothing seems to be happening at all. And yet, over time, it is clear that something is going. And it is this. Gradually, the sense that things are really happening to 'me' weakens, as does the sense that 'I' am really doing anything. What comes to replace it is a sense instead that everything is just happening and to no one. And, because it is not really happening to anyone, the sense that it really matters begins to fade too. All that is left is a sense of whatever seems to be going on, and of it being somehow perfect however it is. So, the sense of something being lacking goes too, and with that the agitation, movement and becoming. That is not to say that all activity stops, all trying to get anywhere. It does not. But it is no longer experienced as really mattering. What results from all this is an enormous relaxation that just seems to deepen over time. It is not a relaxation such as one feels after a holiday or a massage. That is a person feeling more relaxed, in 'this' way or 'that', for instance in the body or more globally. This is rather the relaxation that arises out of the gradual fading away of the whole sense of being a person in the first place. It is the relaxation of the whole system; a massive unwinding of the whole apparent organism.

The way this left me feeling was like a balloon that was a few days old and out of which some of the air had escaped, so that it was no longer taut but instead soft and flaccid. It was as if all the energy had gone out of everything and this became more and more apparent as time passed. I became aware that all the drive that I used to have was no longer there any more. I found I no longer wanted to do anything particularly, both on a large and a small scale. Throughout life I had had a sense of having various plans, projects or ambitions. In part they constituted my sense of having a life. My life was the doing of these projects, the fulfilling of these plans, the striving to achieve these ambitions. Fairly soon after coming back from Wales I realised that all of that had gone, or that the energy had gone out of it all. For example, because I had been painting for many years I had accumulated a lot of work that I had done, oil paintings, gouaches, pastels and charcoal drawings. For many years I had the desire to find a gallery to exhibit this work with the twin hope of off-loading some of it, for it is quite voluminous, but also of possibly earning something of a living from it. And now some time after coming back from Wales I realised that this would never happen, because the drive to do it had gone. There was simply no energy behind it any more. Occasionally, the thought would still be there, when I saw all the piles of work, but the energy behind it was no longer there and so I realised that it would never be more than a thought now. And this is how it was for pretty much everything.

One manifestation of this energy going out of everything comes in relation to need. Need arises largely as a function of the held-sense of being a 'person' and the resultant experience of living out a drama which that creates. This manifests in various ways. To experience oneself as a 'person' is to experience oneself as separate. This sense of separation is often not noticed. What is noticed is the sense that something is lacking. And this gives rise to a felt-need for all sorts of different things in order to try to make good the sense of lack. 'People' feel a need for money, pleasure, power, success, recognition, fame, belonging, acceptance, love and so on and so on. The list will be endless, because the sense of lack for a 'person' is a permanent feature of their experience. So, for example, I used to have a felt-need to exhibit my work. It was something I believed the doing of which would give me a degree of satisfaction and that would make me feel more whole or complete. All of our lives are made up of a myriad of things like this, from the meal in our favourite restaurant, to the holiday we are looking forward to in the summer, the promotion we think we deserve and the pay rise we believe we should get in order to be able to buy that bigger house – which we believe we need. And so on, and so on.

Need also comes to the fore through the drama of being a 'person' in the world. As a 'person', I have my place in the world, surrounded by all the other people and objects. In my interactions with all these other people and things I find myself buffeted around. This buffeting creates suffering for the 'person' because their felt-needs are not met. For instance, if 'I' consider myself to be a decent, upright sort of person and someone treats me with a lack of respect I can feel offended and insulted; my pride can be hurt. This causes me to suffer and out of this experience of suffering comes a need for other people to treat me with respect. This need then leads me into a kind of pushing and pulling relationship with the other people in the world, to try to get the kind of respect that I crave. And this pushing and pulling and the further buffeting that results from it can then create even more suffering and even more need. To deal with this and to ensure that his needs are met and that he does not suffer too much, the 'person' can then end up trying to control his environment, particularly the other people in it. But all the other 'people' in the world are also trying to control their environment to ensure their needs are met too. The result is only continuous and ineliminable conflict. One only needs eyes to see to notice this being played out constantly in the world.

The specific need that is actually experienced is born not out of the general sense of being a 'person', but rather out of the specific held-identity of that 'person' as it has arisen from their conditioning. People, for instance, whose identity is tied up with being powerful and in authority will experience a need to have their power and authority acknowledged, something that people without that identity will not feel. Similarly for people whose identity is tied up with a sense of being generous, or intelligent, or beautiful, or good or whatever else it might be. In each case they will experience a felt-need for that identity to be acknowledged and respected.

Awakening undercuts these various experiences of need by removing the wellsprings from which they arise. The less there is a held-sense of being a 'person' at all the less need is felt for anything so as to make good a sense of lack, because no lack is felt in the first place. Equally, the more the constructed identity of the 'person' crumbles, the less there is a felt-need for others to treat us in a particular way. This has a significant effect on our relationships with others. Our relationships with others can be understood to be grounded, very largely, on an unspoken mutual contract to meet each other's needs. To the extent that there no longer are those needs in the same way the whole pattern of our relationships with others will change. This relaxation removes the neediness out of our relationships, but also their intensity. As with everything else, the energy goes out of them.

This does not mean that there is just indifference and passivity. The organism will still seek to preserve itself. So, if there is hunger there will still be a movement to eat. And if the organism finds itself in a hostile, or threatening, environment it will move to protect itself. Basic functioning still carries on as it did, just without the sense of there being a 'person' there needing those things. What does go is the whole sense of needing things in relation to the whole superstructure of life, jobs, possessions, status, wealth and recognition. Alongside that, what gradually crumbles is an investment in the game-playing aspect of relationships with others, the sense of needing things from them and seeking to meet their needs in turn.

The gradual evaporation of the held-sense of being a person thus leads to a depersonalised experience of life. It is odd in a way to describe it as an experience, because experience is generally taken to require an experiencer. Our whole notion of an experience is that it is something that arises for a 'person'. So, when we talk of an experience of sadness or of seeing a tree that is generally taken to mean that there is someone there who is feeling sad or seeing the tree. In fact, all that ever happens is sadness arising, or tree seeing; as an impersonal happening within the organism. All the different functions of the body-organism, then, continue to occur, just without the sense of a 'person' there experiencing them. So, seeing carries on, also hearing and all the senses. Similarly, feeling and thinking continue as functions, alongside sensation.

This depersonalised sense of the human being as a body-organism rather than a 'person' leads, over time, to a sense of this functioning organism as being more like a machine working rather than a flesh and blood human being, acting, feeling and thinking. This can be quite disconcerting, both in relation to oneself and others. I remember once, a short while after returning from Wales, coming home in the tube in the evening. The carriage was quite full, so I and quite a few other people were standing. Close to me, were a man and a woman talking together. As I looked at them it was suddenly clear that there was no one there. The man's face moved while he talked and it was as clear as daylight to me that this was just happening, like a machine going. As the sounds came out the facial expressions changed, with an attempt to back up and give significance to what was being said. It was quite a complex, co-ordinated performance. What was also clear was that as far as the man was concerned he really was there, and so was she, and what he was talking about was something that was both real and really mattered. The whole situation looked ridiculous, like a couple of puppets on strings dancing around, but somehow convinced that they were real people and were responsible for what they were doing and that it had some real significance.

When the aperture of the camera, as it were, opens wide in awakening what is seen is that behind the manifold separateness, that is taken for reality, is an undifferentiated unity or oneness. It is seen that I am not a real person separate from everything else and with that the sense that anything else is real and separate collapses too. What this brings about is a disintegration of the whole sense of a real, objective world. The apparent separation is just that, an appearance or manifestation. It is not real. In a sense, the seeing of this is what awakening is. It is the corollary of the seeing through of the held-sense of being personally separate. The two are different aspects of the same manifestation.

What this is like is something that ultimately cannot be said. Language is through and through dualistic. If something is black then it is not white. If it is tall then it is not short. How there can be a unity or oneness that transcends all these apparent differences simply cannot be put into words. Words can at best gesture towards it, as a kind of expression, but they cannot describe it. As well as being beyond words and beyond description, it is also really beyond experience. The glimpse, or minor awakening, that happened in Paris was not an experience that I had. I was not there. I seemed to disappear and all there was, was 'that', what I have tried to describe as light, or presence, or the ground of being, but which cannot really be described. When I was back 'that' was gone, but the room I was in and all the things in it were also back again. In this way, a full opening to the reality beyond the subject/object distinction, beyond all differentiations, is not something that we can experience. And this can be seen to be obviously so. *We* are the subject, and with that comes the object necessarily. For there to be an opening to the reality beyond subject and object both have to be seen through, or subrated[6], revealing the deeper reality that underlies these apparent

---

[6]Subration is the traditional Advaita term for the seeing through of something, in which what was first seen to be one thing comes to be seen to be something quite different. The classic example is the snake that is seen in the early morning light that upon closer inspection is seen to be actually a coil of rope. It is not that the snake was real but is no longer. The existence of the snake was only ever a delusion, but so long as we were in thrall to it it seemed quite real. Once it is seen through, however, it is also seen that it never had been real. It always had been a coil of rope. We simply had not seen it.

The process of waking up is traditionally seen as proceeding by the gradual subration of the constructs that form the belief system that support the delusions of personal being, subject and object, space and time, causation and free will, as well as all ideas of normativity – that is good and bad – as well as purpose. The final, instantaneous moment of awakening is the temporary subration of all that forms the held-sense of personal as well as other limited reality.

distinctions. But that is not something that we, as subjects, can ever experience.

Ultimately, then, awakening is something that cannot be said, and cannot even really be experienced and this is true also for the nature of experience that arises after the initial realisation has passed. Something of the experience of a typical human being seems to return, but something of what had been seen also remains. Because of the presence of this element of what had been seen the form of experience that arises out of it cannot also properly be described. It can be gestured towards, turned into some kind of story, but that is all. This is why nothing in this book is really true. Ultimately, it is all about something that cannot be said, the mystery and paradox that is everything.

To look upon the world, after awakening, is to see this mystery. Everything becomes the incarnation of this mystery. The jug no longer looks like a real object, with determinate properties, but instead as a kind of mysterious presence. It has an insubstantial quality, as if it is somehow hollow or empty. It is as if something else is present through it and therefore it no longer seems real as what it is in ordinary experience, a jug. This is not to say that it seems like an illusion. There is still clearly something there it is just no longer the 'real' object that it was always seen as previously. To say that there is still clearly something there is ambiguous, because precisely what goes is the sense that there is really something there, or at least a jug really being there. What there is appears more like a manifestation as a jug, though even that sounds too substantial. It is more like a manifest*ing* as a jug; something that is happening, rather than a thing that is. Everything is a continuous happening or manifesting in that form. There are jug forms and cat forms, tree forms and human forms. There are also fridge motor sound forms, hunger forms and feeling irritated forms. Everything that is experienced is simply a manifesting in that form.

The evaporation of the held-sense of personal being and the gradual shift in experience that comes with that dissolves the whole sense that everything is real. Things seem to take on an 'as if' quality, in which they are apparently happening, but not really so. The more this seems to fill out, the more strange, or even ridiculous, does the apparent experience of a typical human being become. The deeper this goes the more it comes to be seen why awakening is called awakening. It is like waking up out of a dream that is not true. People experience themselves as real and everything else as real. They not only believe, but experience, everything that is happening as happening *to* them. Their lives become a great drama in which everything is experienced really to matter, and to have real significance. To wake up is to see through this dream, to see it as simply a delusion. For some reason, human beings live with this delusion, while nothing else does.

The experience that everything that happens is really happening *to* us makes it feel that whatever is going on really matters. It makes it feel both real and significant, with the result that we are in thrall to it. The traditional meaning of the word 'thrall' is to be a slave. Thus, the modern word to be 'enthralled' really means to be captivated like a slave, by something. That is the real effect of the identification that arises out of the held-sense of being a real person; we end up as a kind of slave to our experience. It is like a dream world that we are in thrall to. With the collapse of the held-sense of personal being, this sense that everything is real and therefore that it really matters is removed and with it the thraldom in which most people live out their lives is seen through for what it is. The effect of this is like the ending of a love affair. The ending of a love affair can sometimes seem like the coming out from under a spell. We can come to see things more clearly for what they really were and realise that we were in part enthralled by something that was not actually real. It can be like that with awakening. The collapse of the sense of a 'person' can have the effect, as its converse, of a falling out of love with the world. Because the whole world no longer seems to be real, but only the form or manifestation of something quite 'other', the whole sense of being fundamentally connected to, and invested in, it goes too. Home is no longer to be found in this world, but in this 'other' that every other apparent thing, as well as myself, actually is. So, it is not just particular things, like a love of history or an interest in visiting museums that go after awakening, but the whole sense of inhering in the world at all. The deeper the collapse of the sense of being a real 'person' the more there is a sense of having fallen out of the world. It is the loss of everything that had made up 'life' previously.

Over time, all that is left is 'what is'. In certain respects this can seem very ordinary, for it is everything - and everything includes some very mundane things. So, it is the cellophane wrapper around the bananas, the chewing gum trodden into the pavement and the dirt in the corner of a tube station platform, just as much as it is the sun setting in glory over the horizon or the panorama of a stunning landscape. It is everything; or to turn that round, there is nothing that is not it.

Space, Time and Causation

Out of the sense of being a person, the experience of living in a story arises. This story is experienced as real and it is the seeming reality of this lived-story that gives life its dramatic quality. Inherent in this lived-story is the experience of time as being real. A story is something that happens through time. It involves movement from one place, with one set of events going on, to another place, with different events occurring, with possibly all sorts of stages along the way. It is a drama through time. The sense of being a person, then, and the thraldom with the lived-story that arises from it, involves an experience of time as real. And this gives rise to a conviction within the human being that it is.

This sense of time as real is undermined after awakening, grounded as it is on the held-sense of being a real 'person'. In the absence of this held-sense, the experience of living in a story or drama gradually ceases. Nothing is experienced really to be happening. Instead it is realised that the sense that it was only arose as an expression of the dream world of being a person. Now, it is seen that there is no movement and no becoming, that nobody is actually going anywhere, no matter how much there might be the experience of it. All there is, is oneness manifesting as everything and this manifesting is happening in a timeless present.

That there is no time means that there is actually no past and no future and so equally no present. What are called the past and the future really only show up as manifestations that are experienced as occurring in what can be called the present moment. The past only exists, for instance, in the form of what is experienced as a present memory. There is the thought in my head of eating breakfast this morning, but that only exists as a thought that is going on, as it were, now. Or, the past can seem to exist because we have something that seems to capture or describe it. For instance, we might have a photo of the Christmas lunch we had with our family last year, or a piece of writing, like a newspaper article, about some event that happened at the other side of the world yesterday. Again, both of these only arise as a manifestation in present experience. The conviction that they refer to a real past only arises out of identification with a narrative, and this narrative is clearly only a construction in thought. For example, someone might look at the photo and remember the Christmas lunch that it is of and all the people who were there and the things that went on. All of that, however, is only a collection of memories and narratives that they are going over to themselves or repeating to someone else and as such it is only a construction in thought.

It is the same with regard to the future. Human beings live their lives as a story or drama that is really happening. This overall story is made up of a vast number of smaller stories; such as, going to the shops, finishing this piece of work before the deadline, helping my child with his homework, booking the next holiday and so on. Each of these stories involves a movement or trajectory from the past to the future and the thraldom that comes with the held-sense of being a person means that both this future and the trajectory towards it come to feel real. So, for example, if I was given this task to do yesterday by my boss and the deadline is tomorrow, then my experience is that the deadline is real, it is something that will really happen, and it really matters. Out of this comes the conviction that I have to meet it with all the drama and pressure that creates. What is actually going on now, in as it were the present, is lost or swallowed up in this movement, or arc, from what is experienced as a real past to a real future.

After returning from Wales, the whole sense of myself as a real 'person' living through time in this way seemed to collapse. With that, things that I had always held onto as having happened in the past to me thereby defining who I was seemed to just disappear. Occasionally memories still arise, but the sense that what they depict is something that really happened to me, in a real past, is largely no longer there. In its place, is a sense of being something that is somehow timeless and without an identity. Whatever happened 'before' simply has no connection to what I now realise I am. This arises from the absence of a held-sense of me being a real person any more and as a result there is no longer the experience of someone being here with a real life, or story, that continues through time, running from the past to the future. In other words, it is the 'person' who is the creator of the past and the future and even of the whole experience of time, including the present, for without the past and the future there is no present either. Talk of 'present experience', then, is not really accurate for there is no present for experience to arise in. This makes it very hard to speak about and describe. One ends up using expressions like the 'timeless present', which appear self-contradictory. All there is is 'what is', and 'what is' simply cannot be put into words. It can be said that it is timeless, but what that means cannot be explained, or even understood.

How this actually manifests is quite odd. At home we have a cat and occasionally he comes through the cat flap and then walks over to his food bowl. Only it does not look like that any more. What it looks like instead is a kind of continual appearance and disappearance out of nothingness. There is not a subsisting thing moving through time, but rather a whole sequence of, as it were, momentary appearances out of nothing. It looks rather magical. He is just 'there', 'there', 'there', without a sense of continuity between the different appearances. The cat appears in this manner as a result of the fact that he moves, in a way that the floorboards and the jug do not, because they are stationary. However, they are appearing continually out of a kind of nothingness in just the same way that the cat does. This is the reason why they have the wondrous quality that they do, because they too are seen as endlessly new, only I am not aware of it in the same way because they do not move.

The visual world, then, so far from opening out onto a world of subsisting objects, is an ever-new manifestation with no continuity. It is only the presence of the held-sense of oneself really being here that grounds a similar sense that everything else is really here as well and it is this that gives rise to the experience of objects subsisting through time. It thereby transforms what actually is a kind of wondrous newness into something familiar, something known and the same as what went before. And this changes it totally. The wonder goes and so too the newness and aliveness. In its place is left something pallid and grey, something that can be manipulated and used, because it is known, but which is eternally dead in our hands as soon as we touch it. The look of a 'person' is like the Midas touch; it turns natural beingness that is endlessly new into lifeless stuff.

One result of this endless newness is that 'what is' never becomes boring. The need for stimulation, therefore, is much less than it was before. When I was young I found the absence of stimulation unbearable. I could not 'be' and there was a chronic sense of lack and of the need for something new to make up the experienced shortfall. As I have got older, this has lessened, but the need for stimulation and distraction remained. All of that has subsided massively since the retreat in Wales. Things now have a freshness or newness about them, so they never become familiar or boring.

Just as the sense of time is a fiction, born out of the held-sense of being a person, so is the sense of space. The common experience of space is grounded on the sense that 'I' am here and 'I' am real, and therefore everything else, like the jug and the teapot, are real too. The world is experienced as being made up of a collection of separate objects that are apart from each other, and this apartness is experienced as the spatial relationship between them. So, I am here, the jug is there and the window behind it is further away.

With the end of the sense of personal separation comes the realisation that what I really am and what other things really are is the same thing. The jug and I are not separate objects, but the expression of the same underlying reality. Really, we are the same undifferentiated reality just appearing to be separate. As a single undifferentiated reality there is not really any spatial relationship there. I am not "here' and the jug 'there', because there is no real apartness here, but instead a unitary whole and such a whole cannot be 'here' and 'there' at the same time. It is the same with everything else. Everything is oneness appearing as whatever it is, and as such there is no apartness to be spatially related, no 'here' or 'there' anywhere to be found. So, there is no space.

This is hard to describe because language is through and through dualistic. For instance, talk of the 'jug and I' refers back to a separateness that is not real. This is why some non-duality speakers refer to 'jug forms' and 'human forms' to make clear that these things are really only oneness appearing to manifest in a particular form. But even that is somewhat misleading for it still implies the reality of the form as a kind of thing. So, for example, a jug form sounds like a different kind of thing to a human form. Actually, however, there are no jug forms or human forms, but only an undifferentiated unity. This unity appears to us as differentiation, in the form of jugs, or teapots or humans, but there is no real separation. Talk of jug forms or human forms then, despite seeming to emphasise their non-reality through the use of the word 'form', still reinforces the sense that they are different things, because they are different forms. Human beings, however enlightened, are continually drawn to talk of things as if there is some real separation because our senses are so formed that they cannot experience the undifferentiated reality but only the apparent separation.

What arises after the seeing through of separation in awakening then is an ambiguous experience, neither one nor apart, but somehow caught in a tension between the two. It is clear that everything is not what it appears to be, which is a discrete object, but actually some kind of infinite expression, a single unitary whole, seamless and complete, but there is still a superficial or apparent apartness. From the fact, however, that everything is seen to be a single, unitary whole it is evident that there is no real space, for there are no two separate things to be spatially related to each other and oneness cannot be spatially related to itself. Oneness is a single undifferentiated whole, containing nothing within itself that could be the locus for a spatial relationship.

Another way to understand this is to look at the different ways by which time and space can be understood. The first is as objective time and objective space. Objective space is like a giant fish tank, made up of x, y and z co-ordinates. Everything has its place within this objective space, defined by its spatial co-ordinates, independent of everything else. In a similar way, objective time can be understood as a time line on which, again, every event occurs at a discrete time independent of the time of all other events. Both objective space and objective time are abstractions, the construction of thought out of and upon the experience of 'oriented' space and time, which are the way space and time are experienced by a 'person'.

Oriented space extends out from and around the subject, or 'person', and is only given in relation to him. So, within oriented space, the place of the jug, for instance, is not given by x, y and z co-ordinates as it is within objective space, but in terms of *my* relationship to it. It is, for example, 'near enough for me to reach', whereas the window behind it is 'out of reach'. This oriented space is not a construction out of my visual sensory experience, for the latter only stretches out in front of me, whereas oriented space extends all around the subject. Wherever you are, in whatever space you are, that space is not experienced to be simply in front of you, but rather will be experienced as extending all around you. So, for example, if you are in a room, that room is not experienced to be just in front of you in the manner of a theatre set, rather you are in the room and the room extends around the back of you as well as stretching out in front of wherever you are. Oriented space, therefore, is grounded below the level of the senses, on the sense that I am a real person and that everything else is real too, including this place where I now am.

In a similar way, oriented time is not an abstract sequence of occurrences independent of each other, but a lived-sense of things happening to 'me', typically moving from past to future. The nature of time, within this phenomenal experience is given in part as an expression of the lived-significance of what is happening and the attention that is given to it because, as the expressions 'time flies when you are having fun' and 'a watched pot never boils' reveal, the experiential nature of oriented time is elastic, and is only given relative to what is going on for the experiencer.

Contrary to the way we tend to think about space and time, objective space and time are never experienced and the only forms of space and time that the 'person' ever experiences are oriented. Objective space and time are only constructions of thought out of this primordial person-centred experience. With awakening there is a crumbling of the sense of being a real 'person' and this brings on the fracturing of the experience of oriented space and time. It only fractures, it does not cease completely, however, because some sense of a locality to experience remains, and with that some sense of a locus in terms of which space and time are given. The timeless, space less reality that is one only appears as a kind of deeper background to everything, one which is present behind the oriented space and time that manifest on the surface of centred and grounded experience.

Alongside space and time, the other central constituent of the sense of an objective reality is causation. This is so constitutive of our whole experience of the world that it is hard to imagine anything without it. Whatever we experience we experience in causal terms; for example, the rain falling, then the seed sprouting and later the crop growing. This is an instance of what can be called linear causation, in which one thing or event seems to cause another thing or event. So the event of the rain falling seems to cause the event of the ground becoming wet and the event of the ground becoming wet seems to cause the event of the seed sprouting and that in turn seems to cause the event of the crop growing.

This whole account, however, presupposes that these events are in some sense real and that they occur apart from each other in real time in some kind of direct relationship. With the seeing through of the sense of the reality of things as well as the time they appear to subsist in, it is seen that this whole picture is simply a construction. Rather than a causal sequence of real events that are really connected together all that actually is are timeless instantiations or appearances, as 'this', 'this', 'this'. For instance, the first 'this' could be described as the rain falling, the next the seed sprouting, and the last the crop growing. Each of these occurs timelessly. That is to say, each one does not in reality appear as part of a temporal sequence moving from the past through the present to the future. We might experience them in that way, but that is something that *we* are doing; it is not what actually occurs. The human brain seems so wired up that it constantly joins things up in this way, creating patterns and relationships; so much so, that we convince ourselves that we are actually experiencing it. When it is seen, however, that there is no real time and so no real past and future it also becomes clear that there are no real linear causal sequences at all, but that what we experience as linear causal sequences are in fact only a structure that we impose on 'what is' but that we do not find there.

This construction that we seem to experience also distorts reality in another way. We experience the rain falling, the seed sprouting and the crop growing as singular events united in linear fashion through time. As well as not really being connected in linear fashion through time they are also not really singular events. So, for instance, the seed sprouting is connected not just to the rain falling but also to the temperature of the air, the absence of mould in the seeds, the seed's DNA and a host of other things. And each of these, in turn, is connected to other 'events'. So the absence of mould is connected to where and how the seed was stored over the winter, how insulated it was from the weather, the severity of the winter, the level of damp present and so forth. And then again, each of these factors is tied to others. So, if the seeds were stored in a barn whether they survived the winter depended in part on whether rodents were present and if so in what numbers, with all the other factors that this depends on. All of these different inter-connected factors are tied together and stretch out horizontally, as it were, to form a single, seamless whole.

This whole as a single, seamless reality takes in the totality of everything that is in the timeless present.

So far, then, from a linear causal sequence, of a singular event A followed by another singular event B and that in turn followed by a further singular event C, what actually occurs is a single, unitary whole as the totality of everything that appears to be in the timeless present, apparently succeeded by another unitary whole in an equally timeless present and then another one and so on. Each of these unitary wholes is 'what is' as a single, timeless appearance. And as such, each appearance is freshly minted, seeming to arise out of an apparent nothingness. It is only thought that connects them together, seeing each unitary whole as arising out of the 'previous' one and abstracting out of these wholes features, in the form of objects and events, that it sees as related together, giving rise to the experience of causation. Actually, nothing is causing anything else. Causation is just another appearance in the dream world of the 'person'. Experientially, when the 'person' is no more it is clear that there is only 'what is' as a single, unitary whole taking in the entirety of everything that appears to be, timelessly and causelessly arising, as it were moment by moment, endlessly fresh and new.

Suffering

The sense that human beings have that time, space and causality are real grounds the lived-sense they have of living in a story, in which one thing is leading to another and all of it is vital and significant. The seeing through of the sense of being a real person that occurs in awakening and the gradual evaporation of the held-sense of being someone that then typically happens, equally gradually undermines the sense of living in a real story. To the same extent that the sense of living in a story falls away what arises in its place is a simple living in 'what is'. It is simple, but also endlessly new and rich. It is not coming from anywhere, nor is it going anywhere. It just is and has a timelessness about it. It is the constant mystery of being appearing as everything.

One result of this is the gradual evaporation of suffering. Suffering is born of an identification with a reality different from that which actually obtains, typically out of a held-sense that things 'should' not be like this, but 'should' be like that instead. These ideas of how it 'should' or 'should not' be are thoughts, but suffering is not the result simply of a thought, or it could be dispelled by simply not thinking that thought any more and that can easily be seen not to work. It arises instead out of a held-resistance to 'what is' and a desire or *need* for it to be different. This derives ultimately from the held-sense I have that I am a real person, together with the particular form of constructed identity that fills it out. What causes suffering in one person with a particular constructed identity will therefore be different from what causes suffering in a different person with a quite different constructed identity. So, a person for example who has experienced cruelty in their own life might be unable to accept the reality of cruelty in the world, either towards other people or animals. Hearing about either might cause them to suffer in a way that it would not another person who has never experienced real cruelty. Such a person might not like the fact that there is cruelty in the world, but they will not be unable to accept the reality that there is, and so they will not suffer from it as a consequence.

Suffering is not pain. Pain naturally arises in certain situations. It is a sensation, or feeling, that naturally arises and then falls away again. Suffering is not a feeling, but a state, and therefore it does not just naturally arise and then fall away again, but continues, as long as the identification with reality being different from how it actually is carries on. It can be days, weeks, months, years, even decades.

Suffering starts out as pain. Something happens that causes 'us' pain, something that is experienced as having happened to 'me'. Because of how painful we find it something in us cannot accept it and so we have the thought that it 'should' not have happened, that reality 'should' be different from that. Essentially, suffering arises out of a delusion that reality could, and should, be different from how it actually is. But reality is what it is. To deny reality and say that it should not be as it is is to set ourselves against reality. And that is a struggle we will inevitably lose. There is no way to change reality; reality just is what it is. We may not like it, but that will not change how it is. To battle against it only creates suffering for ourselves. In that suffering the pain, which originally arose in us out of the way reality was, does not go. It does not go because we are resisting it and saying that it should not be like this or should not have been like this. Therefore, it just carries on, for as long as the resistance continues. The original situation could have ended long ago, weeks, months, years, even decades ago, but if we still resist the reality that it happened we will continue to suffer.

The whole of suffering then is a creation of the self, out of its held-sense of identity and what that identity needs and its refusal to accept things that cause pain to that identity. Anything that I feel that I need can, and probably will at some point, lead me to suffer. This happens quite straightforwardly because if I need things to be a certain way and they are not like that then it will give rise to a pain in me that I will not be able to accept, because of my held-need for things to be otherwise.

For this reason, there is nothing the self can do to end its own suffering. The self in part constitutes itself. To be a human being with a held-sense of identity, then, is to suffer. It is intrinsic to the human condition.

The seeing through of the sense of being a person that occurs in awakening and the gradual evaporation that takes place afterwards of the whole held-sense of being a real person has, as one of its side effects, the gradual ending of suffering. This is not something that anyone does, and nor could they. It is simply a natural consequence of the thinning out of the sense of identity that results initially from awakening and then gradually deepens with time. The more the sense of impersonal being fills out, the less there is a tendency to suffer.

Freedom and Loss

Alongside the lessening of a tendency to suffer, the deepening of the sense of impersonal being also brings on a deepening and widening of a sense of freedom. This is a quite different sense of freedom from that which is felt straight after awakening. In the initial aftermath of the retreat in Wales I no longer felt defined by the constructed sense of identity that was Nigel Wentworth and this brought an instant freedom from the inhibition that had always been part of the constructed identity of that character.

This is quite different from what arises later or at least it has been 'here'. The more the held-sense of 'me' has evaporated, the more the sense that everything is one has filled out through life. It is the sense of something like a quiet presence, in the form of everything, from the apples in their plastic wrapper with the sunlight reflecting off it, to the old, rather worn table they are sitting on and the whirring of the fridge motor in the background. It is not them, but what is present as them, or in that form. The less 'I' am, the more this sense of oneness as 'what is' comes to be all there is and with that comes a beautiful freedom. It is not a lack of inhibition, or a freedom of action in any way. Rather, it is the freedom of just being, the freedom that comes with being outside of all stories, all sense of becoming, all time. It is the freedom that arises from dwelling in 'what is', when there is no longer an investment in *how* things are, whether good or bad, pleasurable or painful, easy or hard, and therefore there is the simple experience of the *beingness* of everything. This freedom does not go because 'what is' is always there, except when 'me' comes back with its identification with one outcome rather than another in the apparent flow.

This is the direction in which awakening eventually tends, the simple living of 'what is' whatever that is. That is not, however, how it begins. Awakening begins, instead, with a dramatic shift that brings with it the complete seeing through of the sense of being a person. But it is precisely this sense of being a real person that has formed the core and substance of the whole of life previously. What inevitably follows, then, is a gradual, but inexorable, process of loss. It is the loss of everything that pertains to the individual, to 'me'. Over time it gradually weakens, crumbles and evaporates. The result is a slow shift from personal to impersonal being. This impersonal being, which is all there ever is, or was in fact, only manifests however through the loss of the sense of the personal. The whole held-sense of being a person then has to go, and with that the whole constructed sense of identity that fills it out and gives it form.

Alongside, or as part of that, is the loss of everything that was previously believed to be true. It is the loss of the belief that there is a real world, and that this world is full of real people, of whom I am one. It is the loss of the belief that these people, like 'me', have real lives and things really happen to them, some of which are 'good' and some 'bad'. It is the loss of the belief that we all relate together and these relationships are real, as is the suffering that arises so often out of them. It is the loss of the belief that like 'me' they all have free will and choice and can act so as to try to make their life-experience 'better' and that, moreover, they and I can act in the world to make the overall situation in the world 'better'.

This is a lot to lose. And that is what awakening becomes: it is the total loss of everything that 'you' ever felt that you had and were.

Awakening, then, is not something that you get, or that even happens to you. It is, rather, the end of 'you'. This is not something that a person can understand until it happens. The self only knows the world of its habitation; it can imagine nothing else. But the dream that the self has, that it can remain what it is, the same person that it is, with all its material and non-material possessions, *and* become awakened, that never happens. It is the ultimate irony and paradox; that everything has to be lost in order for everything to be gained.

Awakening is not a special state that a person can be in, then, in the way that it is typically thought to be. It is not about 'being here now', or 'being in the place of the witness', or 'being mindful', or any of the other things that are sometimes said of it. Nobody ever becomes awakened because it is not something that happens to a 'person' at all. Therefore, there is no state that is the state of being awakened for a 'person' to attain to. Awakening is actually nothing to do with the 'person'. It is not the 'person' who wakes up, but rather the opposite, the waking up from the dream, or delusion, of being a 'person'. It is waking up to the reality that there never was a 'person' in the first place.

Another way of understanding awakening is that it is waking up to the reality that actually all is one and there is no separation. There only is 'what is'. Therefore, there is no 'better' place to get to and so nothing to do. Whatever *is*, is oneness manifesting as that, and that is all there is. There is nothing else, there never was anything else and never will be anything else. Oneness never goes. It cannot, because it is everything anyway. Therefore, nothing needs to be done to reach it, because it is already here. It is already everything that *is*.

Chapter Four

The Divine

A week after returning from Wales, I was sitting at the table working very early one morning when I noticed that the jug, the glass, the reflections in the water, the mat the jug was sitting on, everything on the table in fact, seemed to be trembling or radiating with a kind of presence. It was something quite different from anything that I had ever experienced before. It might sound strange, but looking at them, it seemed clear that what was present as them was the divine. At first, it felt almost normal and perfectly fine. There was no sense of intention or purpose about it, but it felt infinitely generous, and had a warmth and softness about it. It was like a loving radiance that somehow seemed to make everything tremble.

This was during the time when I was not sleeping very much and waking at 3.30 or 4 each morning. I carried on working for a while and then went to have a bath. Everything there was the same, apart from now it had a different quality. The softness had gone and instead there was what I can only describe as a kind of radiant majesty. The bathroom sink with its old taps somehow was the divine majesty incarnate and in its presence there arose in me a feeling of utter humility. This gradually became more and more intense. The more majestic the sink became the more humbled I felt. I had always thought of it previously as 'just' a sink, and the taps as 'just' taps. And now they were revealing themselves as this awe-inspiring incarnation. It felt almost like an accusation towards me, for my enormous, puffed-up arrogance, in having thought before that 'I' was something special while these things were mere 'objects'. After a while, this sense of humility became so strong I found it overwhelming. I ended up on the floor, in a Muslim prayer position, offering up complete submission and contrition. I could not abase myself enough and whenever my sense of self-consciousness returned I felt terrible.

Again, after a while, I do not know how long, I began to find it too much to cope with and felt that I had to get away and out of the house and so I went for a walk. But now everything in the street was this too, the lamp-posts, the pavement, the telegraph poles and wires. I walked around a couple of blocks before I came to a street with some small cottage-like houses on the edge of Epping Forest. As I looked at them it was clear that they were not separate houses at all, but somehow the divine manifesting as all of them at the same time. They, as it, were alive, radiantly alive with a full-on sense of majesty. By now this sense of divine majesty was overwhelming, with a stern, forbidding quality about it. It was as if the houses, the church at the end of the road, the lamp-posts and everything else in the street were looking back at me. They were full of this radiant, awe-inspiring and increasingly terrifying majesty and I was there as this worm-like creature who had previously felt myself to be somehow so superior to all of them.

By this stage, I was feeling frankly frightened by it all and struggling to cope. I began to feel that if this went on much longer something in me would snap. I started to want it to end, for everything just to go back to 'normal'. I walked on, looking at the ground so as not to see the houses and the church staring back at me, until I got to the Forest. There, in a way that I do not understand and cannot begin to describe, the trees were understanding and forgiving and with that it all gradually began to feel alright again. Soon after that, it all seemed to stop and everything did at last go back to 'normal'.

After I got home, I went to bed, basically to hide. I felt completely unnerved and frightened and all I wanted was for this not to come back again. I spent most of the next twenty-four hours in bed hardly daring to look at anything, in case it started to look back at me, until I was sure that it really was over and was not returning.

This is hard to write about and I do not like talking about it. Somehow it feels almost profane. It is central to the message of this book, however, so something about it has to be said; though whatever I write will be hopelessly inadequate, because what happened was completely indescribable. No words could ever describe what that was like. Language is framed to describe what makes up what passes for normality. It simply cannot describe things like that.

One of the most powerful aspects of the whole experience was that it all felt to be 'out there', as it were, and that I was not part of it at all. Everything else seemed to be the divine incarnation but not me. Instead, I felt utterly apart and unworthy. It was as if my whole previous existence up to that point had been the denial of the reality that opened up and so I could not feel myself to be a part of it. Intrinsic to that previous existence was the sense, the lived-sense, that ordinary things like the jug, the glass, the table-mat, the bathroom sink and the houses were all just mere objects. And the other side of all that was that I, as a person, was somehow more important. I had never previously seen how much that world-view was embedded in every moment of my experience. Somehow, through that time, and the whole experience went on for two to three hours, it was brutally clear the extent to which it was, with the result that I simply did not feel part of this divine presence at all.

The other thing that was so powerful during that time was the sense of presence. In a sense, that was the whole of it: an opening up to the reality of divine presence as everything. Nothing feels more right than to describe it as a presence and yet it was utterly impersonal, not a thing at all, let alone a being. I do not understand it and cannot explain it; but to experience it was to be in the presence of it, in all its awe and majesty.

In this, it was quite different from the experience of oneness being everything, for instance the jug, or the cellophane wrapper round the bananas or the whirring of the fridge motor. That is more like the absence of a sense of difference or separation between things, a sense that ultimately everything is the same thing only appearing to be different. The experience of the divine as everything was very much of a presence, some*thing*, as it were, being everything, alive, animate, awesome.

The whole experience when I thought about it later appeared to be very much like a traditional religious experience. The first thing that came to mind was Paul on the road to Damascus. This felt very strange, because I have never been conventionally religious at all and have never felt drawn to Christianity. The other side of that was that this was not something that I had ever heard Tony Parsons talk about and I did not know what he would say about it. It felt, however, to be the deepest and most powerful opening onto the nature of reality that I had ever been made witness to and I knew that I could not deny it or accept that it was just some kind of delusion or hallucination. So, I hesitated to ring Tony about it, thinking that this could end up being the parting of the ways for me and him. When eventually, a couple of weeks later, I did ring him to talk about it he immediately understood, as he always seemed to. He described it as a deepening and said that it was something that sometimes happened to people, but not often. He went on to say that this experience and the experience of oneness as everything is really an opening onto the same reality. It is just that the former, because of its nature, is so overwhelming that it cannot be lived all the time. The experience of oneness as everything is a kind of low-level version of the same thing, he said, low-level enough that it can be lived constantly, without it bringing on a sense that one is going mad. He also said that it sounded like a traditional religious experience and added that ultimately everyone is talking about the same thing. He was wonderful and by the end of conversation I was reassured.

Personal and Non-Dual Perspectives

The main immediate effect of what had happened was a kind of levelling of everything, in the form of a realisation that nothing in the manifestation is really higher or lower than anything else. The whole human sense that somehow we are more important than everything else, than animals, plants and stones, I came to see is a complete delusion. After what opened up that November morning, there was a complete collapse of any sense of hierarchy. Before, I realised, I used to experience myself and everything else in egocentric and anthropocentric terms. In my experience, I came at the centre, then other people, starting with those closest to me, then other life forms, starting with the animals closest to man and then plants and finally inanimate objects. The effect of that Sunday morning was to turn the whole of that picture on its head. Nothing now seemed higher or lower than anything else. Everything appeared to have equal significance, or rather insignificance. It was clear that whatever happened to me was no more significant than what happened to a beetle.

This brought to an end in me what can be called homocentric thinking, the thinking according to which what happens to people somehow matters more than what happens to anything else. We justify this prejudice to ourselves in various ways, for instance by saying that we are more conscious than anything else, that we are more intelligent, that we suffer to a higher degree or that we are more creative. We have all sorts of justifications for it. All of that is based, ultimately, on the held-sense that we are real in the first place and that as real 'people' we have these real characteristics. The seeing through of that, the complete seeing through of it, in the perception that actually everything was equally the presence of the divine as whatever it appeared to be completely removed for me any sense of superiority. For how can something that is actually only a manifestation of something else be more important than another thing that is equally only a manifestation of the same thing? If all there is is the divine, if that is the single, unitary reality, manifesting as everything that appears to be, then no aspect of that manifestation has any more significance than any other.

This was not, however, how I had experienced it previously. Feeling somehow superior to everything else, I had felt entirely justified in using everything else for my own purposes and in experiencing those things as somehow existing *for* me. This, I now came to see, had been reinforced by the whole sense of separation that I had always felt, that had made everything in my experience somehow feel limited and inadequate. This had the effect of making everything else feel not just like objects, but 'mere' objects. Because we experience things like trees and stones and doors as 'mere' objects and therefore ultimately limited and inadequate, we experience them as simply available to us for us to use and manipulate in order to make things 'better' for ourselves and feel entirely justified in doing so. That was what I had done and I could see that it was what other people were doing too. This is not to say that there is anything really 'wrong' with that. Human beings doing that, behaving in that way towards everything else around them, is as much the expression of the divine as anything else. It is just born out of the held-sense that something quite different is going on, the real improvement of life-experience by real people who are somehow really superior. All of that I now came to see was an utter delusion.

Another result of the levelling that resulted from this experience was the realisation that whether people behave in this 'exploitative' way or whether they behave more 'responsibly' does not change anything on an ultimate or metaphysical level. This was the levelling of outcomes; the seeing that all outcomes are really the same and that therefore there is no reason ultimately – in terms of what is really happening – to prefer one to another. However deluded the human way of being is, treating everything else in existence as being there for us, to use for our own well-being, there was nothing really wrong with it and things would not really be better were it to stop.

This shift in perspective and awareness happened straight after that Sunday early in November. The full effect of it, however, took a long time to percolate through, as it were. Part of the reason why it took so long to work through, I think, was because my immediate experience was that what had opened up that morning was something 'other' and that I was somehow apart from it. I found this difficult and felt a great desire to be that too and to live it. It felt strange, very strange, for everything to have opened up and revealed itself in that way and yet for me to feel somehow apart from it all. But what was going on 'here' seemed to make that impossible, for there was still far too strong a sense of me being there as a real person. The proof of that was in this very desire itself; something in me still wanted to have what had opened up, to live it, to be it. This was the usual expression of arrogance and self-seeking that characterises all the impulses of the self. I was still experiencing myself as a person and thinking that somehow I could change things in the world and get myself to a better place. It was also the expression of ignorance for, despite everything that had been made clear, I was still assuming that there was a better place to get to and that the divine was not equally everything and so no better or worse outcome was actual or even possible. I could not see that at the time, however, and felt somewhat disorientated that something as profound as that could open up and yet I could still remain experientially apart. What I could not see at the time was that there was no way for a person to live this; and only a week on from coming back from Wales, despite the shift that had occurred there, there was still a strong held-sense of 'me' as a real person. At the time, I could see quite clearly what had seemed to fall away of the 'person' Nigel Wentworth, which had been quite a lot, not the mass of what was left.

It took a long time for this to change and for the crumbling of what was left to occur to the extent that it has. As it did so, what manifested, not just intellectually, but also on a lived level, was a completely different sense of what divine reality was and the relationship of human beings to it from anything I had previously believed or experienced. People conventionally believe that only one way of being is the expression of the living of divine reality, which is to be profoundly calm and loving, like the Buddha or Jesus. Other ways of being are somehow considered lesser. What became clear over time to me, however, was the complete opposite; that everything and therefore all ways of being are all equally the expression of the divine. All the wars, all the brutality, all the greed and ignorance are the expression of that, just as much as all the kindness and peacefulness. There is nothing that is not this. The most brutal dictator or torturer is just as much the manifestation of the divine as the most enlightened sage or saint. It is all really the same thing and only appears radically different to human beings because of the way these different manifestations impact upon us.

Part of what came out of this shift was that I came to see that whether I woke up or not, or became any more aware, really did not matter. Before going to Wales, I believed that me waking up was the most important thing that could happen, though I never believed that it was likely. After coming back from the retreat in Wales it was clear that there never had been a person who could wake up in the first place, the whole idea of a person waking up was a delusion. Over time, after this experience in November, this gradually deepened but also, because of what had occurred, my understanding of this process changed. At first, this occurred through a deepening of the sense that it really did not matter what happened to me, or anyone else for that matter. If everything is really the divine, which had become manifest that morning in November, then a human being who has not woken up is an expression of the same underlying reality as one who apparently has. They are both manifestations of the same reality. So, it is irrelevant in absolute terms, whether anyone wakes up or not. It is only in the relative experience of a 'person' that it seems to matter, for in the story of a 'person' nothing seems to make a greater difference.

This changed my perspective on non-duality and other forms of spiritual teaching. In emphasising the possibility of there occurring a waking up from the delusion of being a person, teachers were still, however subtly, reinforcing the sense that awakening matters and therefore that what results from it is somehow 'better' than what was before. In reality, it is only more pleasant in the experience of the human being within whom the waking up seems to occur. From an absolute perspective, an awakened or unawakened human being is exactly the same thing. They are both just the divine manifesting in that form. What this gradually opened up was an entirely different perspective, no longer about me or another person waking up, but about dwelling in the reality that everything is the divine, not as some kind of 'better' place to get to, but as the reality of 'what is', whatever that happens to be. It is the realisation that everything, really everything, is the divine and therefore there is nowhere 'better' that needs to be got to and therefore nothing that needs to be done.

Obviously, dwelling in the reality that everything is the manifestation of the divine is not something that a 'person' does, or can do. Anything a 'person' *does* is an expression of personal becoming and therefore a reaffirmation of their sense that they are real and so is everything else and that by using their free will and choice they can get to a 'better' place. Therefore, nothing a 'person' does can ever remove them from the realm of their experience, which is the living out of their own 'personal' reality. So, from the perspective of a 'person' it can never be seen or lived that everything is the divine. Dwelling in the reality of the divine expression arises rather through a sinking back into beingness, the beingness out of which the sense of being a person arose in the first place, and this obviously arises by no one's doing and for no one.

That this sinking back into beingness is not something that happens to a 'person', because there is no such thing, means that the divine is, as it were, simply coming back into alignment with itself. The divine was never really estranged from itself, because it is everything, the 'person' who is convinced of their own reality as much as the enlightened sage. But in some way, in the manifestation that is a 'person' there is an absence of alignment, the expression of which is like a wrong note, and again in some way there is a natural pulling back towards re-alignment, in which there would be, as it were, a single note sounding without anything jarring. What is experienced as resonance before awakening is this natural pull back towards realignment. It is the expression of that within us which knows all this already, which knows that the whole world of the 'person' is not really what we are and that there has always been something else, something immeasurable, which has been lost. It is this that appears to be within us calling us home, but is in fact something utterly 'other' coming home to itself.

This coming home to itself continues after awakening. Awakening is not the end of the process, but at most the beginning of the end. A vast clearing out of all the conditioned clutter takes place thereafter. This clearing out has an inexorable feel about it, as if it is unstoppable. There is no sense of 'me' driving it. In fact, it could not feel less like that. Rather, it feels like something entirely 'other' that having gained a foothold within the form starts to expand outwards until it has filled and transformed the entirety of what was once a 'person'. To describe it in that way makes it sound like an intentional process, as if something is directing it, and that is not right. But at the same time there is a sense as if of some force drawing everything deeper into itself, similar to how it is when one stands on the seashore as the tide is going out and one can feel the pull of the water drawing one to go with it. In a similar way, one can almost feel the pull of this 'otherness', drawing one into it. Doing things that are not concordant with this sensed-reality feels increasingly difficult and eventually unbearable and there is consequently increasing resistance to them. There is simply a stronger and stronger pull to be here and stay here.

The image that repeatedly came to mind during this time and also later was of being like a glass of water into which a drop of red dye had been dropped. At first, the drop of ink just swirls around in the centre of the glass, leaving most of the water untouched. Then gradually, very gradually, it begins to defuse through the water. The more it does so the more the previously clear water turns red. Eventually, if left long enough, all the water in the glass will turn a lighter colour of red. This is what I felt to be going on within me. I could no more make it happen than stop it from happening. It just seemed to be occurring inexorably.

What results from this is not a new identity for the person, because precisely what is realised (in both senses of the word) is the reality that what is appearing as this human being is in fact only the divine. What emerges over time, then, is not something that can have either this identity or any other. Rather there is only a gradual sinking into an increasing sense of personal nothingness. The converse of this is the filling out of a sense of boundlessness, of everything partaking of the same underlying reality including oneself, the very opposite of a sense of personal identity.

The more this process deepened, the more it became apparent to me that it was not so much that awakening did not matter, as that it was simply not real at all. It does not really happen. The whole conventional idea of awakening presupposes a person who wakes up. The realisation that all there is really is the divine – the realisation that there are no real people at all, not in any sense of the word – is the realisation that there really is nothing to wake up and that consequently awakening does not really happen. All that actually happens is that within the whole manifestation that is everything, that aspect of the manifestation which is the sense, or experience, of two-ness or apartness, as it were 'here', falls away. Both this sense of two-ness or apartness, and the sense of location 'here', however, are only an appearance. They are not real. There never was any real separation or division and there never was anything that was 'here' as it were and not equally as much 'there'. The sense of them both only ever was a delusion. The end of them, then, is only the end of an apparent delusion, it is not anything that is really happening at all. Before, there was only the divine manifesting as everything and afterwards there is only the divine manifesting as everything. Nothing has actually changed at all.

The result is that the shift that happened in Wales, which at the time seemed like the most important thing that had ever happened in my life, eventually came to seem ultimately irrelevant and even trivial. It was only ever 'me' who saw any significance in it and the more the sense of 'me' has crumbled away the more anything that ever happened to me has come to seem really quite unimportant. It is all quite comical and to think of it makes me smile; at the puffed-up vanity of a person – myself – really believing that what happens to me actually matters.

Over time I have come to understand this shift as being from a personal perspective to what could be called a perspective of non-dual reality. Before I went to Wales, what happened to me and what my experience was like seemed vital and significant. I identified with it and a lot of energy went into trying to make that experience as 'good' as possible. This investment in 'me' and 'mine' was seen through in Wales, giving rise to a lived sense of what can be termed the impersonal reality – that there is really no such thing as a separate person with free will and choice and that actually everything just happens. In a sense, this is what awakening is, the awakening from the delusion of being a real person. What opened up after this November morning was a whole new dimension, no longer concerned with the reality or otherwise of the person, but rather with the deeper non-dual reality that everything that appears to be is the unitary manifestation of the divine. Despite this non-dual perspective opening up something of the personal perspective still remained, only gradually crumbling away over time as the held-sense of me as a real person has gradually evaporated. As it has done, in its place has arisen a sense of everything as being equally an expression of the same unitary reality and therefore of no particular thing, including my experience, having any more significance than anything else.

What arose out of this was a tendency to be pulled in two rather contradictory directions at the same time. The more I came to see everything as a unitary manifestation of the divine the more how things were within my experience came to seem quite unimportant and even irrelevant. On the other hand, something of the personal perspective remained, giving rise to a desire to remain attuned to this experience and increasing resistance to whatever drew me away from it. This tension was to remain unresolved for a long time.

The Kingdom of Heaven

After the weekend in Pax Lodge, I have described how over the course of the next few days even the most ordinary things seemed to take on a wondrous quality. It was as if each thing was new and I had never seen it before. Things seemed to have a presence and radiated a kind of aliveness that was wondrous. At first, this was just the way individual things were, or features of individual things, like the texture of something. This wondrous quality was there whenever I happened to look at something. When I was not looking at anything in particular, but just absorbed in the flow of life, it tended to be absent. But as soon as the flow stopped and I happened to look at something it was there again.

It was as if a gap had opened up somewhere in the fabric of the world and a wondrous light was shining through. At first, the gap was very small and only individual things, or the features of individual things, appeared in the light. But gradually, very gradually, it seemed to open out. It stopped being just individual things and the features of individual things and became collections of things, such as all the things on the table by the window in the room where I work. I cannot remember how it progressed after that, but eventually, much, much later, it became everything. Just sitting here, now, everything has that quality, all the things, the shadows, the colours, the light, the sounds, just everything. It is as if the whole world has been transfigured and everything has an alive presence and sense of wondrousness.

I do not remember when, again, but at some point I was so overcome by the radiance of everything that I found myself thinking that it was like the kingdom of heaven. I do not know why but the phrase just came into my mind. And then it suddenly seemed obvious that this is what Jesus had been talking about. To see this wondrous presence in everything is to be in a kind of heaven. It is beautiful beyond anything that humans are able to create. No painting has the same wondrous perfection as even the most ordinary thing when it is seen for what it really is. It truly is perfect and there is no sense ever of anything needing to be different. Whatever is, as this presence, is perfect in that form, whatever the colour, the texture, the material, whether it is natural or man-made. It is all the same and in its simple presence and beingness everything is radiantly perfect.

It is radiant, but strangely still at the same time. Things have a sense about them as if they have always been that, whatever it is and however it is, and could never be otherwise. Everything therefore seems timeless. Being timeless there is no movement to it. Instead, it is as if everything has come from nowhere and is going nowhere. Everything just *is*. Somehow this is-ness or beingness has a quality of profound aliveness, but is also utterly still and silent at the same time. It also has a kind of softness about it, as whatever it appears to be, even things we normally think of as hard, like metal or concrete. For a long time, as I have said, this sense of everything as a wondrous, still presence full of radiant softness was only in individual things, or collections of things. And for a long time it remained only visual. Only much later did it become things in movement or things that are sensed via other senses than sight. Now, the cat moving on my lap is that too, as is the sound of the fridge motor whirring away in the background.

It felt strange when I first had the thought that this is what Jesus had been talking about when he spoke of the kingdom of heaven, for I have never been conventionally religious, let alone a Christian. I have always found the institution of the Church alienating; its services, words and rituals. None of it has ever really chimed with me. There have been times when I wished that it would, but it never did. Most fundamentally, I found the whole idea of a separate divinity, one with apparent intention, impossible to understand or accept. Since the glimpse in Paris, it has been clear to me that ultimately everything was one and therefore to the extent that there was anything sacred it was also clear that it was not apart from everything, but *was* everything. So, the idea of a higher sacred divinity separate from and above the non-sacred world seemed profoundly wrong. Moreover, even the message of Jesus, that one 'should love one's neighbour as oneself' did not resonate with me. It just sounded to me just like another 'should', another morality, telling the self how it needed to behave. I could also not see how anyone could be loving in this way. From my own experience it seemed clear that the self could only really love itself and act in its own self-interest, even when it was apparently acting for another. So, loving one's neighbour as oneself was simply something human beings could not do. Real love also never seemed to me something that someone has to try to do. Any love that results from a person trying to love, because that is what they feel they 'should' do, is not really love at all. Moreover, all the love that human beings seem to have within them seemed to me to be ultimately conditional. The kind of unconditional love that Jesus seemed to be talking about just did not seem possible for human beings. For all these reasons, I had never felt at all Christian, yet now I found myself realising that when Jesus talked about the kingdom of heaven, he had been talking about exactly what I was now experiencing. It was quite disconcerting and shook something deep within me.

This sense of being shaken out of myself only deepened when, over time, it gradually became clear that the kingdom of heaven was not just a wondrous and soft presence but was also full of love. The teapot sitting on the mat and the texture of the towel hanging on the radiator are both a loving presence. They have an endless loving patience and seem to look back at me from that place. The kingdom of heaven is a realm of pure love, as everything that *is*. Everything is that. It is a love beyond words and beyond understanding. It both is love and draws forth love. To be in the kingdom is to be in love, to inhabit love, to breath love. It is an intoxication expressing and drawing forth a profound stillness and quiet, like the sound of a single bell played upon the soul. There is the appearance of things happening, of sounds, movement, feelings and thoughts, but behind it all there is the sense of profound quiet and stillness. Describing it like this seems so inadequate. Words can never grasp it, for the unknowable cannot be described. In the same way, it cannot really be seen or experienced, for it is not any*thing*. But somehow, magically, it can make itself apparent through, or behind, everything that does appear to be, an infinity being finite, a timelessness being now and an endlessness being here. It is the beingness of everything, as the incarnation of divine presence and the expression of unconditional love.

The other thing that gradually became clear was that this softness and quiet, this sense of stillness and belonging is always there. It is not this that ever goes, but me that loses touch with it. When 'I' am there, experiencing myself as a separate self, as separate from everything, I cannot experience it, and so become estranged from it. But the kingdom of heaven is actually all around us all the time –

everything is the kingdom of heaven – it is just that we do not experience it. As Jesus said, 'The father's kingdom is spread out upon the earth, and people do not see it.'[7] There is something tragic, but also comical, about the fact that we live in paradise, but because we cannot see it we go around searching for it throughout our lives.

In a sense, there is only the kingdom. That is all that is real. Everything that exists is in that the whole time, including people; it is just that because we feel real and so separate from everything we do not see it. And the more we react to our experience of alienation by trying to grasp at things the more cut off and alone we feel. For the kingdom to be lived, the self has to be absent, for the sense of 'personal' reality and apartness banishes the kingdom. And the larger the self, the more aggrandised it becomes, the more protected, reinforced and defended, the more alone and unhappy we become, because we end up feeling more and more separate and so more and more estranged from the kingdom that is our natural inherence. The complete melting away of the sense of a separate self would be to dwell constantly in the kingdom, but we are so terrified of letting go, of becoming nothing, of being nothing, that we cling to our wretched little sense of ourselves and make our lives a misery as a result. We have traded the kingdom of heaven for a delusional sense of self that never was and never can be. It has given us mastery over the planet and inner misery.

What this also means is that the kingdom is always there. It is not the kingdom that goes, it is we who become blind to it. Therefore, it is also true that it has always been there, that it always has been the reality. We always have been in the kingdom of heaven we just did not know it. It is as if we go around with special glasses on that somehow stop us from experiencing things as they really are. And because we do, and so cannot experience the kingdom, we go endlessly looking for it, when actually it always was everything anyway, so there was no need to go anywhere, or do anything at all to find it in the first place. The tragedy of it is that out of our sense of lack we think we need endlessly more of something in order to

---

[7]M. Meyer *The Gospel of St Thomas* Harper/Collins. 1992. saying 113. p63.

make up for the held-sense of deficiency and this endless striving for more of everything is leading us to despoil the whole planet in the search for the wholeness we believe we have lost and which would be ours again, if we could but stop grasping for it.

This is another paradox; that we live in paradise but, because we feel real and so apart, we cannot see it and so go off searching for it. It cannot be found, because it was never lost and already *is*. It is like looking for the front door keys when actually you have them on you in your back pocket. It does not matter how hard you look, how much of the house you rummage through, or even turn completely upside down, you will never find them, because they were never lost in the first place. It is the same with the kingdom. As Jesus said, 'The kingdom is like a person who had a treasure hidden in his field and did not know it.'[8] It was never lost. It is everything that already is, whatever that is. If you tell yourself that it is not 'this' whatever that present reality is and so go off looking for it, trying to get to somewhere different, somewhere better, you will never find it. This is because it is not over there or tomorrow, but here and now. The present wordless reality, whatever it is, is that.

Many people I believe see something of this but persuade themselves that it is not it and so pass on. I think that I did that myself when I was quite young and the detour it led me on, until I got back to the same place again, took over thirty years.

Out of this sense of the kingdom of heaven as an incarnate presence came the realisation that actually everything is animate. This was seen in its full radiance on that November day, but it has inevitably and thankfully faded from that intensity. Gradually, however, it came back, but in a much more subtle and gentle form as the experience of everything as the kingdom. There is a quiet aliveness to everything, whatever it is. It is not that the cellophane wrapper round the bananas is itself alive, but rather that it is the manifestation, or realisation, of something utterly 'other' that is. All

---

[8]M. Meyer *The Gospel of St Thomas* Harper/Collins. 1992. saying 109. p.63.

things, all the things that appear to be, that is everything within the manifestation, partake of that same aliveness. Stones, the teapot, the floorboards, they are all animate, all equally alive.

The Divine and the Absolute

At some point, a long time later, I realised that what I had experienced and was calling the divine was not the same as what is referred to in Advaita[9] as the absolute. For me the divine was what was on that November morning when it was clear that there was a presence, at first gentle but later majestic and awesome, that was in some extraordinary way manifesting as everything that appeared to be. It was completely clear that all the multiplicity, all the differentiation, was in fact a unity, a singular unitary presence of some*thing* as all the things which to me appeared to be, all the houses, lamp posts, paving stones, basins, trees and clouds and it was this 'thing' – as it were for it was not a thing at all in the way that other things are things – or this underlying reality that I have referred to as the divine.

At the time in November it seemed odd that the divine could be there manifesting as everything and yet I could still be there seeing it. In this way it was quite different from what had occurred when I was sitting on the floor in Paris when the whole of the phenomenal world and phenomenal experience seemed for a timeless time to be suspended. *I* did not see the 'light' or 'presence', to use two inadequate words for it, for I was not there any more, nor did this 'light' or 'presence' have any location or attribute, for the whole phenomenal world disappeared too. In Paris it had seemed as if this 'otherness' could only become manifest through the temporary suspension of the whole of subject/object experience, that form of

---

[9] Advaita means 'not two'. Advaita Vedanta is a branch of Hinduism that asserts the non-dual nature of reality and identifies the individual self (atman) with the ground of reality (Brahman).

experience in which we are there and so are all the other usual things that for us make up the world.

On that November morning, it was clear that what was manifesting as everything that makes up this world was not itself another thing within this world – in that sense it was entirely 'other' – but somehow it was also the ground or reality behind everything that was. In some extraordinary way, that was completely beyond understanding this 'otherness', that instilled in me at first reverence and then awe and finally a kind of terror, was everything that in this world appeared to be whilst at the same time itself being of a quite different order of reality. That, whatever it was, was real – ultimately, awesomely real – whilst all the forms that it appeared as were only that, an appearance.

What had seemed extraordinary at the time was that all of this could open up and yet I could still be there looking at it, as it were. How could something that transcended the phenomenal realm and phenomenal experience be *seen*, and that is to say how could something that was beyond the phenomenal world still seem to appear within phenomenal experience? At the time, I remember being struck by the extraordinariness of it all but did not think much further about it. It was only much later that I realised that my being there witnessing 'it', as it were, create or be the world in front of my eyes meant that however awesome and majestic the divine presence had been for me that morning it was a different dimension of reality to what is called the absolute. The absolute is that; absolute. It is beyond all distinctions, all differentiation, all multiplicity, all division and so all experience[10]. The absolute cannot be experienced and so nor can it be known. Nothing can be said of it of a positive nature at all. All that can be said are negative things, that it is 'not this' and 'not that'; not that it 'is this', or 'is that'. The absolute it can be said is not limited, not bound, not in space and time and beyond all experience and knowing. But it cannot be said that it *is* anything at all. Though I had no understanding of it at the time, it was this

---

[10] This is a basic tenet of Advaita philosophy; that the absolute (Brahman) is beyond all differentiation.

reality that had somehow opened up when I was sitting on the floor in Paris. After whatever happened was over and I was back sitting on the floor again I had used the words 'presence' or 'light' or 'the ground of being' to describe what was, as it were, once I and the world were no longer there. But it was clear even as I did so that these words did not remotely describe what that was. No words could, for it was beyond all categories and distinctions. It was ineffable.

As such, what opened up while I was sitting on the floor in Paris was closer to what is understood as the absolute than what became manifest on that November morning. On that morning, what was seen was the way the apparent multiplicity is generated out of a singularity of absolute 'otherness'. The world that human beings live in, in which everything within our experience seems real, has never been so clearly seen to be actually only a dream world, for it was completely clear that actually all of it was only an appearance or manifestation, out of 'otherness', and so not real at all. The reality behind it, the reality it was the temporary, apparent or experiential, instantiation of, was actually of a totally different order of being, one that it was clear was is unknowable and indescribable. All that can be described is the phenomenal experience of it, which could best be described by such words as 'majestic', 'awesome' and 'terrifying'.

This is not to say the absolute and the divine are not identical. The absolute and the divine are the same reality, just under what for want of a better word could be called different 'modes'. The absolute is that about which nothing positive can be said, to which nothing can be attributed. The divine is the same reality, but in that mode as which it manifests as everything that appears to be. The two are ontologically identical, the same singular, unitary reality, but we apprehend them differently. The absolute is beyond all experience and we cannot know it at all in any positive sense, the divine, by contrast, can be apprehended, though only through an unknowing and revelatory experience, in which it reveals itself as the creator of the apparent world.

The Divine and the Relative or Phenomenal World

On that morning in November, what was seen, for as long as it lasted, was that everything that formed part of my experience was really a kind of manifestation of the divine. After it was over, however, everything appeared to go back to 'normal'. The table was a table again, and the chair a chair. And that in itself seemed quite strange. How could something go from being the expression or incarnation of radiant majesty to appearing to be just an ordinary chair again? I did not know. Nor is it completely true that everything seemed quite ordinary again. Before, everything had looked real, so a tree was a real tree and a chair a real chair. For a few hours it had all been seen through almost completely and now when the seeming ordinariness was back again it had a quite different quality about it. Somehow, nothing felt completely 'normal' any more and it never has again since. It is as if something of the sense of reality that everything has in the dream world drained out of it on that morning. At first, all there was, was something of an empty blank. The world of people, houses, trees and traffic was there again in its apparent normality, but the reality had drained out of it and with that all of its vitality. It took a long time for that to change, but eventually this blankness or deadness has been replaced by a aliveness that is everywhere palpable. The jug of water and all the other things on the table now radiate this divine presence, only with infinite softness. The jug can still be used to pour water, but it is clear that is not what it really is, a mere thing for carrying water. It now has a presence, as something quite 'other' in that form, which is indescribable and the source of endless wonder.

The seeing of everything as full of divine radiance or as the manifestation of the divine raises the question of the relationship between this manifestation and that which manifests as it. Is the way things manifest, as a jug, or a bathroom sink, or houses in the street, merely an appearance and so not real at all, with only that which is manifesting being real, or is the manifestation in some sense both real and unreal at the same time? In part, this depends upon the perspective. From a relative perspective the manifestation is both real and unreal. From this perspective, the jug in front of me is real, because it holds water and I can pick it up and pour water from it. So, it is not unreal, like an hallucination or delusion. At the same time, though, it is clear that it is not really a mere thing to be used, but somehow the incarnation of divinity in that form. Something of this ambiguity is how I believe things are typically lived after awakening. Things, like jugs, are still related to in a way as if they are real, because they are still used in the normal way. But there is no longer the sense of reality about it all and it is clear that something quite wondrous is continually occurring. This is not to say that there is a continuous living of this 'otherness', human beings simply cannot live in that or they would go mad. What actually arises, then, is something more manageable, the more prosaic seeing that everything is oneness appearing in that form, but without the full-on experience of divine presence and majesty. And in that form things can be said to appear to be both real and unreal.

From an absolute perspective, however, nothing is really as it appears to be in the manifestation, for in the manifestation there is the experience of apparent separateness and in reality there is no separation. From an absolute perspective, then, the manifestation is simply that, an appearance; there is nothing real about it. The way reality is simply cannot be known or experienced; for any way in which it could be said to be, or even experienced to be, would have to be in a particular form, as 'this' and therefore as not 'that' and that is dualism. Moreover, to assert that the manifestation is real in any way is to say that both that which manifests and the form in which it does so are both real and that is again dualistic. Ultimately, the nature of reality in itself is beyond knowing and simply cannot be understood. To try to go beyond this is to get into metaphysical speculation; and that would probably only end in a contradiction, because words are limited and the divine is not.

That the things that appear to manifest are not real means that all there is, is the single, unitary manifestation that is the divine presence as everything that appears to be. This everything is a seamless whole. The divine manifests not in the form of separate things like a jug, and a cat, and a fridge motor whirring, but rather as a single unitary whole, in whatever complete form that whole appears to manifest in that apparent instant. To put it another way, there is only a single, unitary manifestation in the timeless present, as it were, 'now', 'now', 'now'.

Eventually, this leads to an awareness that there only really is the divine constantly manifest*ing* as whatever appears to be. That is to say, actually there is no being, but only a vast doing, the timeless doing by the divine that is everything that appears or manifests. Rather than nouns, what are needed are verbs, for everything is really only a doing. So, the 'jug' is really the divine jug-ing, the 'cat' the divine cat-ing, the 'fridge motor whirring' only the divine fridge motor whirr-ing. And what sees and hears all that is only the divine human-ing in the form of see-ing and hear-ing. There is no one here doing the see-ing or hear-ing; they are just apparent functions, more manifestings of the divine presence.

Sometimes it is argued that this kind of radical non-dualism involves the denial of the relative, in that it says that all that really is is the absolute or the divine. It is true that there is only the divine, but the divine is what appears to us as the relative. From a human perspective, and that is the only perspective we have or ever will have, the divine is only known through the manifestation. The complete denial of the relative would therefore be the complete denial of the divine or the absolute. The relative is the absolute and the absolute is the relative, only in a way that we cannot begin to understand. It is only implicit in the word 'relative' that it is not ultimately real.

All that is, then, is the endless mystery that is everything that appears to be. And over time what this turns into is something akin to the simple living of that mystery. The certain reality, that was the dream world, in which everything seems hard and real, gradually disintegrates and in its place arises the soft, silent mystery that is endlessly manifesting.

Any attempt to grasp this only distorts it. Words can never describe it and the human mind cannot encompass it. Any attempt to even discuss it or write about it seems to force it into a shape that is unnatural, distorting it in the process. It can be approached from many angles and each will seem to have a certain validity from there. It can be talked about as 'being rather than becoming', 'a manifestation rather than reality', or 'an arising in experience as opposed to the seeing of a real object', and so on. But from a wider perspective it can be seen that all these attempts to describe it are mutually incompatible and ultimately inadequate and that none of them are really true. They are stories that we tell ourselves, to try to make sense of the endless mystery that is 'what is'. But ultimately, none of them get further than silence.

All that comes to be left, then, is the living of everything as a manifesting. It is everything in the sense of all the particular things that seem to be: the line, half lost in shadow, where a pencil meets a table and the grain of the wood of the table that it lies on; the hum of an aeroplane flying over London in the sky somewhere and the hard sensation of the floorboards under my feet as I sit here. It is not just neutral or pleasant things that come to be lived as this. Things that are experienced as unpleasant or difficult are it too, for instance, things going wrong at work, being barged in the street or being caught in the rain and getting soaked.

It is not really, however, the whole collection of particular things that arise in life that comes to be experienced as 'everything'. To talk of it in that way again implies that these apparent things exist apart from each other, each a separate thing in itself. What arises, in fact, is quite the opposite; the sense of a whole, of which each particular thing is actually only an apparent manifesting. Or, to put it another way, there is in fact only oneness. Oneness as a pencil lying on a table, with the line between them lost in shadow, oneness as the hum of an aeroplane flying overhead, oneness as being barged in the street. Rather than describing this as everything being oneness or the divine, it is closer to how it is experienced to describe it as oneness or the divine being everything.

This amounts to the coming into being of an experience of a reality below or behind the level of how things superficially appear.

It is the realisation that everything that appears to be is actually only a manifesting. In a sense, it is the realisation that nothing is real, at least in the way it used to appear to be. A pencil lying on a table before seemed to be a real pencil lying on a real table. Now it seems like something entirely 'other' appearing in the form of a pencil lying on a table. What now seems real in that is whatever is doing the appearing; the appearance is only that, an appearance. This does not mean that the appearance is unreal, only that it is simply an appearance. An appearance is an actual appearance for us, it is not an hallucination or a delusion, but it is still only an appearance.

Once it is seen that everything is oneness, or the divine, appearing as that, it also becomes clear that ultimately everything is the same. The pencil lying on the table is the divine appearing as that, so is the glass half full of water. The two are therefore the same reality. Everything really is the same reality. Or, to put it another way; there is really only one single unitary reality. The pencil lying on the table is not one thing and the glass half full of water another. They are the same unitary reality only appearing in apparently separate forms. The same with the sensation of hardness below my feet, or the hum of the aeroplane. They are all different manifestings of the same deeper reality.

This can sound odd, but when it is seen it seems quite obvious. Apparently different things come to have the same timbre, as it were. It is as if the same quality is radiating through them all. It is hard to describe beyond this, for anything that is said will only distort it in some way. But, if I were to try to describe it, I would describe this quality as a kind of stillness, or silence. There is a stillness in all the apparent motion, all the hustle and bustle, all the seeming change. Equally, there is a seeming silence behind all the apparent sounds. These are just words, but it is something like this quality that has opened up since that November morning, gradually filling out more and more, until eventually it has become everything. It radiates through everything, and it does so equally as a form of stillness or silence *being* everything.

The Non-Dual Reality

The shift in perspective that comes with this is enormous. It is like the complete turning upside down of everything. Prior to the retreat in Wales the sense I had of everything was based on the held-sense that I was real and therefore so was everything else. And because all these other real things seemed separate, they were therefore really separate. So, the glass full of water was a real glass full of water and the pencil on the table was a real pencil on a real table. And because they were both real they were both different things, separate from each other. Moreover, because everything was real it all seemed significant. What happened seemed really to matter and from that arose a sense of drama, of things really happening to me. And because I experienced things as really happening to me I was always reacting to them to try to make them more as I thought they 'should' be or as I needed them to be. All of this has gradually disintegrated and in its place has arisen a completely different sense of how everything is.

The main change has been the gradual arising of a simple sense of everything simply being a manifesting. There is only 'what is', however that is, and whatever it is it is all ultimately the same thing. Because it is all experienced as being the same resistance towards it has gradually crumbled. Over time, the whole sense that some things are 'better' than others has weakened and atrophied and as it has done so a sense that nothing needs to be different from how it is has arisen. This is not because it is experienced to be wonderful as it is. That would again only be the expression of a personal perspective, that things are just fine the way they are; basically just fine for the 'person'. This has nothing to do with a person experiencing the way things are as just fine or even wonderful. Rather, it is to do with what could be called a non-dual perspective arising within which it is seen that because it is all really the same thing not only could it not be different from how it is it does not need to be either, however that manifests in experience for the person. So, something that is going on that is experienced to be difficult for me is no longer seen as 'wrong' and therefore as needing to be different to the extent that it was. It just is, in the same way that other things that are more pleasant just are, and there is no longer the same resistance to things being like that.

The other side of this reduction of resistance to things is the arising of a natural going along with everything. The pushing and pulling that characterises the relationship of a 'person' to everything largely stops. Even things that previously seemed impossible to accept come to be experienced as somehow strangely perfect, without any effort for it to be like that. Again, this has nothing to do with a 'person' making himself accept things, by trying to be more 'accepting'. It is simply a natural going-with things that arises without effort, because everything is experienced as just being as it is, and therefore not needing to be different.

Another effect of the seeing of the world as only an appearance, or as an apparent world, is the gradual draining away of the interest that used to be in it. The interest, which was there before awakening, arose from it seeming real and vital. Everything that happened seemed to be really happening to me and therefore it seemed really to matter. If things went in a way that I experienced as 'better' that seemed to be something of real importance, similarly if it went in a way that I experienced as 'worse'. With the seeing that it is really all the same thing anyway, all of that melts away. Nothing is really better and nothing is really worse. Nothing really matters, for it is all actually the same thing anyway. Interest in the world, then, largely drains away, both on a 'macro' and 'micro' scale.

On a macro scale, this manifests as the collapse of the sense that things really need to be different in the world. I was brought up in a political family, not only with a sense that what happened in the world really mattered, but also that it was possible, and important, to engage with it and try to make it 'better'. All of this has now largely gone. Most fundamentally, the whole sense, that was so strong before, that things could really be better one way rather than another has steadily weakened. Oneness cannot be improved. It is perfect however it is and however human beings happen to experience it. Even something as enormous as global warming no longer really seems to matter. Even if the world warms up to the point where most life on earth, including that of human beings, is largely wiped out, that will still be oneness only in a different form and it will still be perfect. That might sound callous or inhuman; and from a human, personal, perspective it is. The whole point is that this is not a human or personal perspective. From a non-dual perspective everything is simply one. It is not more one in this form than that one. It is not more one if global warming does not happen and people survive than if it does and they do not. It is in fact exactly the same reality either way. And because these two are essentially the same thing, what reason is there to prefer one to the other? It is all perfect, however it is, because it is all the same divine reality.

From a personal perspective everything is experienced in terms of meaning. Nothing is value-neutral. Nothing just 'is'. Everything is either 'good' or 'bad', 'better' or 'worse', 'beautiful' or 'ugly'. What happened on that November morning was the seeing through of this perspective. It was the seeing that everything is really one and therefore nothing really has the meaning that people attribute to it. What had previously looked like two separate houses it was clear was actually a singular, unitary manifestation only in the form of two separate houses. That form was not real and so nor were any of the qualities that appeared with it, for instance that the old Victorian front doors were 'attractive', or that the plastic windows were 'ugly'. Nothing is really attractive or ugly. With that can come the thought that ultimately everything is meaningless and it is sometimes talked about within non-duality circles in that way. To describe it in that way, however, is still to be thinking within the structures of meaning, which are ultimately human and personal. This is because for something to be meaningless there has to be something else that is meaningful and the whole point of what is being said is that nothing really has the meaning that human beings attribute to it. So, it is not that things are meaningless, any more than they are meaningful, it is that the categories of meaning simply do not apply to how everything really is. The categories of meaning are a human construction. They have been framed in terms of our human, all too human, purposes; that is to say, to enable us to order and arrange things as we believe they need to be in order to make our held-stories as good as possible.

Outside of that context, they simply have no application. Oneness, therefore, is neither meaningful nor meaningless. It just *is*.

The draining away of a sense of normativity as real did not just undermine interest in the world on a macro level, but also on a micro level, in terms of my own life. Whether what happens goes this way or that, whether it actually happens at all or not, increasingly simply does not seem to matter very much. As a result, interest in the world, in the sense of the world that I live in, has also largely drained away. That does not mean that there is indifference. If it is raining I will put a coat on. But the sense that any of it really matters has gone. It is sometimes said that after awakening everything still carries on, it is just that there is no longer the sense of anybody doing it any more. That is true, up to a point, though it is a fairly limited point. Yes, if I am cold I will still put a jumper on, with it now being clear that that is something that just happens and that 'I' am not doing it. A lot of the basic things in life like this still carry on, but a lot of the larger fabric that made up 'my' life has not just carried on, only without a sense of 'me' doing it, at all. As a result of the collapse of the sense that what is happening is really happening to 'me' so much of the investment in my life has simply fallen away. Therefore, quite a lot of what previously made up that life has fallen away with it. At the beginning, it was things like my interest in history and visiting museums that seemed to go overnight. Over time, however, much else has gone too, for instance a desire to socialise. The reason for this is that so much of what goes on between people seems to be a sharing of each other's stories as a way of each person gaining reassurance and support in their experience of these stories. With the loss of investment in the sense that I have a real story going on, the desire to share it with someone else has largely evaporated and with that the interest in meeting up very much in the first place. Another thing that has gradually evaporated is a desire to listen to music. I used to listen to Radio 3 quite a lot and also to go to concerts and operas. All of that has gradually stopped over time. Ordinary sounds, like the fridge motor whirring or the clock ticking, anything really, are the kingdom of heaven in the same way as the jug of water on the table or the texture of the wood beneath. The need for other sounds, like the sounds of humanly made music, is simply not there any more.

What has opened out since that November morning has also gradually changed my whole perspective on this process. At first, it seemed like the most important thing that this process completed, that I woke up fully, whatever that means. I would feel frustrated when I realised that I had gone back into experiencing everything as a 'person' again and would feel a level of satisfaction when I realised that something else had been seen through or had fallen away. Eventually, all that has gone too as I came to see that what happened to me, or how things were within my experience simply did not matter. However it was, it was all the same divine reality anyway. Whether I was seeing everything as simply a manifestation of oneness, or whether I was going back into identification with personal experience, I came to see that it was all really the same thing and therefore it was not better one way or the other. How could one thing be really better than another, when actually they are the same thing? As a consequence, my resistance to it being one way or the other, particularly to my going back into identification with personal experience, began to weaken and lessen. Paradoxically, this shift, from a personal to a non-dual perspective, seemed to come at the same time as a much deeper abiding in the sense of everything as the divine manifesting and therefore with a lessening of the tendency to go back into experiencing everything from a personal perspective in the first place.

This shift also made the apparent things that go on in the world seem fundamentally different. If everything that appeared to be is a unitary whole of absolute 'otherness' then the apparent changes that take place to things are not actually happening at all. If I move the apparent glass from one 'place' to another, so that its 'spatial' relation to the apparent jug appears to change that is not actually a real change at all, for there is still only everything as the same unitary whole. On the level of absolute 'otherness' nothing has changed at all. This was completely clear on that morning in November. Any 'changes' that took place to the 'houses' was no change at all *as* the divine. As the instantiation or realisation of the divine nothing ever changes. Everything is always that. It is a single, unitary whole, changeless and unchanging.

What this means is that the events which make up the drama of human life are not just not happening *to* anyone, they are not really happening at all. The sense that they are not happening *to* anyone can be called the impersonal reality, the reality that is seen when it is realised that there are no actual people. Obviously, if there are no real people then nothing is happening to anyone, because there is no one for it to happen to. The reality that nothing is really happening at all is the non-dual reality, the reality that all there is, is a kind of singularity, being the divine or oneness manifesting as everything that appears to be. That is to say, because the events that appear to make up the drama of human life are actually only an appearance of absolute 'otherness' in that form, and this absolute 'otherness' is a changeless whole, these events are not really happening at all. Whatever apparent events occur are only the apparent expression of the divine, they have no reality in their own right. The divine is undivided and unchanging. So, the apparent events and happenings in this world, that to us are the most real thing in the world, are only a kind of appearance. They are not really happening at all. It is only for human beings, with our particular make up – our brains, our senses, our bodies, our socialisation – that things appear in the way that they do. We make the mistake, however, of taking how things appear to us for reality, when in fact it is only an insubstantial dream.

This has never been as clear as it was that Sunday morning. At times it is clearer, at times it seems to subside and apparent separateness and apartness come back more to the fore. When it is clearer what is seen is that there is only this unitary manifestation. As the expression of absolute 'otherness' it has no past and no future, and no story. It just *is*, as everything that appears to be. As such, the chair and the sound of the fridge motor are not two separate things, but aspects of a single expression. It is timeless and space less. There is no 'before' and no 'after', no 'nearer' or 'further', for it is all the same thing timelessly being. It is a solid, still, timeless whole, going nowhere.

This sense that everything is a kind of no-thing going nowhere arises the more the sense of time as real seems to fold down upon itself until there is only the timeless present. Similarly, the sense of a solid, still, whole arises the more the sense of separateness and spatiality evaporates. All that is left is a sense of a vast stillness going nowhere.

From this, it also becomes clear that as everything that appears to be is only a manifestation of absolute 'otherness' and this 'otherness' is timeless being, then the apparent arising and falling away of things in the appearance is only that, an appearance. Nothing and no one is really ever born and nothing and no one ever really dies, for nothing in the relative or phenomenal world is real at all. Personal death, then, is a delusion. What we call death and experience as personal death is simply a change in the form in which the divine appears to be manifesting. Nothing more.

Being the Divine

It took a long time to happen, but eventually I realised that the divine was everything that I appeared to be as well. This sounds like the most egotistical thing to say, but in fact it is the opposite. It was the realisation that there was no real 'me' and that everything that was 'here' was really only an expression of the divine. I was not a person, with free will and choice, deciding what I did. Instead, like everything else, I was empty of inherent being and just a manifestation of divine being. Everything that arises 'here', everything that I do, is only that, however I might experience it or behave at times.

With this came the sense that not only did I not need to be different in any way from the way that I was, but that I could not be. Everything just is, unavoidably the way it is. Nothing could be different. To sense this is to experience everything as a kind of concrete whole, solid and unalterable. In this realisation, the impulses that make up 'me' seem absent and there is only the living in the flow of 'what is', unavoidable, inevitable and somehow perfect.

This brought with it a change to my sense of home. At first, after I returned from Wales there was a sense of having come back home to a place where I realised I had always been, only I had not previously been able to see it. There is still something of that, something of the sense that the reality of 'what is' which makes it home has always been there, right in front of me and that I was always looking at it, only that somehow, for some reason, I missed it or looked past it. But, now the sense is not just of having stopped looking past this reality, but of the nature of this reality being fundamentally inverted. What this has opened up seems so vast, so enormous, so different and so indescribable that it no longer feels very connected to what I had somehow always sensed to be the nature of things. As such, home now feels like quite a different place from the home that I suddenly found myself back in after the retreat in Wales. Then, I felt that home had been found again, after many years adrift, wandering in a world that felt alien and apart. That sense of home still involved some sense of something that had found home or come home only it was no longer experienced as a real person, because for a 'person' there is no home but only permanent exile. Home now is the completely impersonal sense of unity, completeness or wholeness that is the divine manifesting as everything that appears to be. In that sense, it does not really feel right to call it home at all, for the very notion of home seems to imply a being, or something, that can be there and this is the very opposite of that. The divine is home to nothing, for there is nothing else but it in existence.

This unity or wholeness that is the divine manifesting takes in the world but is not of it. That was manifestly clear on that November morning. As a result, though the sense of alienation from the world that has been there most of my adult life has gone, it has not done so through me becoming reconciled to the world, coming to experience worldliness as normal, but rather through the world ceasing to seem real and becoming instead simply a manifestation. 'What is' is the radiance of absolute 'otherness', and it is that 'otherness' that has become home. The world is only the form in which it seems to appear.

The realisation that one is the divine is also the loss of any sense of being 'this' or 'that', that is to say, of having any particular quality or nature oneself.   For if what the divine is itself is simply unknowable, or a mystery, then to realise that that is what one is, too, is to realise that one is only that mystery also.   The living of this sense of mystery brings with it an openness and with that openness comes a sense of freedom and joy.   This is not the freedom of a 'person' who feels able to do what he wants. It is in fact precisely the opposite, the freedom *from* the sense of being a person with all the conditioned habits and reflexes that come with it.

The other thing that becomes clear over time is that alongside the natural joy and sense of well-being that is there in the absence of the held-sense of being a real person, is a natural outflowing of love. The way that this manifests has also changed over time. After the retreat in Wales, there was a full-on sense of love for everybody that made me want to hug everyone I saw. That gradually settled back into a gentler lovingness that was not *for* anything, or anyone, in particular. It was just there, in the same way as the sense of well-being and joy was there, as something that just seemed to bubble up out of nowhere and for no particular reason.

This came as rather a surprise to me, as I have never been a particularly loving person, as people who know me would probably testify. From the age of fifteen I was perpetually caught up in a sense of struggle, either to do with my own sense of anguish at being here at all, or with practical difficulties that arose through life. That sense of struggle came with a constant movement *to* somewhere, either somewhere known or not-known, but always away from here, wherever I happened to be or whatever happened to be going on. That kind of movement of becoming precludes a natural lovingness, for in the movement to become the sense of one's own beingness is lost and this love arises from that place. Becoming is of the 'person', and a 'person' cannot love in this way, for a 'person' knows nothing but the cycle of his own lack and his seeking to find something to make good that sense of lack.   Whatever love a 'person' feels is ultimately self-love. There is no space for genuine love of another, because everything is the expression of the sense of lack and self-seeking. It is only when there is no more any sense of separation and therefore of lack, that love can arise, as a natural feeling and outflowing, for no one and no for reason in particular.

As this love is not an expression of the 'self' 'here', nor is it directed towards any other 'self' 'there'. That is to say, it is not the love of a 'person', nor is it the love for a 'person'. It is just love. It is as much for the pear tree, or the wood pigeons in the garden, or the floorboards on the floor, as it is for any human being. There is no sense that humans are more worthy of this love, or that it is more appropriate for it to be there in relation to them, than in relation to anything else. This love arises equally for everything. It knows no hierarchy of worthiness.

This is another paradox. So long as we are caught up in the struggle of a 'person', believing that some things are 'better' than others, for instance that love is better than anger, or peace better than war, we are always trying to get to somewhere else, to this place that we think is 'better'. So, if we think that love is 'better' than anger, we might try to be more loving and less angry. That trying, however, that effort on our part, is also the denial of 'what is', for if we notice that we are angry we will resist it, because we will see it as 'wrong'. That struggle, that effort, that resistance, means that we are in constant movement away from beingness and into becoming. And therefore, we lose touch with our natural way of being, which is to be loving. It is only when there is an openness to 'what is' equally, however it is, that the struggle and resistance stops and the love that we naturally are can be. So, it is only when we see that everything that makes up 'what is' is equally it, which is to say that the hatred and war is as much the divine expression as love and peace, that we stop pushing and pulling at everything. And it is only then that our own natural lovingness is able to come to the fore.

I say 'our own natural lovingness', but it is not 'mine' or 'yours'. 'You' or 'I' can never feel this love, for it is not of a 'person'. This love only is when the 'person' is no longer there. Or, because these things are not black and white, this love only is the more the sense of being a 'person' has evaporated. Thus, when 'we' are absent, when seeking has stopped and when there is just our natural beingness, then this love flows naturally.

Arising out of our beingness it is quite different from the love of a 'person' for another 'person'. It has none of the needy, grasping, conditional quality that people call love. This love asks for nothing, needs nothing and is affected by nothing. It is not noisy or shrill. It does not call attention to itself. It is, rather, a still, quiet quality, like the sound of a bell. It does not belong to anyone and no one has it, or feels it. So, it is not 'my' love, or 'yours'. It is just love, from no one, for no one or for nothing. As such, it does not result from any effort. It just is and flows naturally in the absence of self-seeking.

Moreover, because it is not 'mine', not of 'me', and because it is an unconditional upflowing for no one and nothing in particular, it has nothing to do with liking. This kind of love is there as much for people one would not like, or things one finds ugly, as it is for people we find congenial or things we find attractive. It manifests, then, in quite the opposite way to the love of a 'person' that is entirely conditional on liking and approval. The two are so different that it seems a mistake to call them by the same name.

As well as being the nature of our own beingness, it is also seen to be the nature of everything else too, that is, from the cellophane wrapper round the bananas to the dirt in the underground. Everything radiates a quiet love, when no 'one' is there any more seeking anything. Somehow, love is the nature of all beingness, and all beingness is love. As such, love is the expression of the divine. The absolute 'otherness' that is everything is, somehow, unconditional love in the form of whatever it appears to be. And that includes all the wars, all the hatred and all the ugliness that man has created for himself to live in. It is all the divine manifesting as that, and it is all equally the expression of absolute, unconditional love.

Chapter Five

After Awakening

After returning from Wales, I have said that there was not an immediate collapse of the sense of being a 'person'. Instead, certain aspects of what had formerly felt to be 'me' seemed to go, while others remained. A long period of to-ing and fro-ing then ensued between more personal and impersonal ways of being. Eventually the times in which the character Nigel Wentworth returned became less frequent, and also weaker in intensity. To some extent, the shift just happened slowly and imperceptibly, so that without anything appearing to have happened in the interval I would at some point become aware that something that used to occur no longer did, or not in the same way. This was quite strange to observe, as it was as if aspects of my character or behaviour were just gradually crumbling or dissolving. But there were also more definite shifts that seemed to occur at particular and what seemed like random times. These were like the aftershocks to the original earthquake that had been the opening up in Wales.

January

The first occurred in January, several months after the retreat in

Wales. During these months there had been a gradual widening in the sense of the wondrousness of things that began after Pax Lodge. At first, this had only been experienced in relation to individual things, but it gradually widened becoming first groups of things and then larger ensembles. It still felt very much 'out there', however, and I continued not to feel part of it. It was quite strange, in that there was a sense of having come home after Wales, but this sense of things as wondrous, as the incarnation, or expression, of the divine, somehow did not include me. It was as if two rather fundamental shifts had taken place that were clearly connected, but somehow did not join up. At the time, I did not question it. It was simply how it was. It is only now, looking back at it, after it has all changed and moved on so much, that it looks strange that it could have been like that.

It carried on like this for a few months until something more seemed to shift after which I no longer felt apart from the manifestation but to some extent as much 'it' as everything else. It was set off by something that occurred one day when I happened to be on my way back from the fish shop. I had gone to buy some fish for dinner and on the way back I was thinking about all the things that brought 'me' back, all the triggers that set off a reaction in me that brought the character Nigel back. And suddenly I had a kind of sudden flood of insight or clarity. It was as if something opened up, or a light was shone on something that had always been there but had always been obscure and now suddenly it was completely visible. I saw in a different way to the way I ever had before that it was all to do with me going around with a sense of myself as a real person with a real identity. Anything that threatened that sense of identity triggered a reaction. At the same time, it was suddenly obvious that I was not really that identity; this identity was simply an identity that I happened to have because of where I had been born, my family upbringing and so on. I could see that if the same body-organism had been born in a different culture, or at a different time, it would have had a quite different identity. My identity was in a way arbitrary and not what I really was. Instead, what I really was, was this 'otherness' that is the divine in exactly the same way as everything else. My identity, then, was not what I really was, but was instead more like a set of clothes that I just happened to go around wearing. Somehow, I had got into identifying with them as if they were really me when they were not. In an instant, it was all completely clear. It was as if a veil had been removed and things that had always been obscure before were now laid out in front of me and I could see straight through them. There was a realisation that I had been living this fiction, that 'I' was this real 'person' with the identity of Nigel Wentworth and that this had been going on all my life. And now suddenly it was seen through. As well as being completely clear it also seemed so absurd. 'I' had been taking offence at insults directed at an identity that was not what I really was. 'I' had been trying to protect the interests of an identity that was not me. 'I' had gone around for years imagining myself to be someone, the character Nigel Wentworth, looking at everything through the eyes of that character, trying to defend the interests of that character, when actually it was not what I really was. This was just an assumed identity; it was not what I really was at all, any more than the leaves were real leaves and the jug was a real jug. All of that was just the manifestation of something quite 'other' appearing as that. And so was I.

In that instant, something seemed to pop. It was as if something of the sense of me being a real person had somehow survived the minor awakening in Paris and even the much greater awakening in Wales but had now suddenly been seen through; and somehow, having been seen through so clearly, it could no longer be maintained in the same way. At first, I could not stop myself laughing. It all seemed so absurd, the ridiculous charade that I had been carrying on for years, of being a real 'person', with a real identity and trying to protect myself and fight my corner in the world. It just made me laugh. But that soon changed. Over the next few days, I found myself experiencing an aching sense of sadness. At the same time, I now also began to feel myself a part of the divine expression in the same way as everything else, the floorboards, the table, the jug. It was clear it was all really the same thing, including me. This was all that I had ever wanted; an end to the sense of separation and apartness, to the sense of being cast out, and with that the experience of being home again. And yet, now when that sense of being home seemed to be filling out, it brought up an enormous and deep sense of sadness. With the sadness came an aching sense of loss. It was as if someone I really cared about, or loved, had just died or gone away and I knew that I would never see them again. I felt so awful I just wanted to lie down and grieve. It was not just about losing 'me', but also of losing everything that 'I' had or was attached to or was in some kind of relationship with. Moreover, it was not just about the death of 'me', but also of 'everyone' else too, because if I was not a real person nor was anyone else. And if my identity was just a construct, so was everybody else's as well. If what appeared as 'my' life was actually just an impersonal manifestation of something utterly 'other', then so was 'everybody' else's too. Really, I did not have a life and nor did anybody else. It was all just a vast impersonal happening, going nowhere. The enormity of it all loomed up and I felt completely bereft. The dying, as it were, of 'me' was not just the end of that artificial identity that I had been trying to protect, but also of the whole of what constituted personal life, the web of relations with everybody else within which that identity functioned.

I felt punctured, empty and flat. For a few days, there was a terrible sense of sadness. And then just as suddenly everything felt completely fine again. It was as if the loss had never really happened and everything was perfect just as it was and always had been. Thinking about it, it sounds odd or implausible, but at the time it did not feel strange. It all just felt completely fine and there was no sense that it had ever been otherwise. Something similar to this happened several times over the next year. Some kind of shift would occur and I would feel that part of 'me' was going, that something was dying inside me or was being let go of. Each time there was an aching sense of sadness and loss for a short time, followed by a feeling of complete well-being as if it had never happened. It was as if the collapse, or crumbling, of a part of the constructed sense of identity felt like an acute loss at the time it happened but then, as soon as it was over everything would go back to being somehow whole and perfect again, because whatever had gone was not what I really was and never had been. Within a few days each time I would feel as if nothing of significance had happened, that nothing of significance had gone or been lost and I could not imagine how I

143

could ever have found it difficult. It always felt quite odd, how it was possible to go through such intense emotions and then for them to disappear so quickly and completely. But that was how it was.

With this shift in January, a few months after coming back from Wales, came an end to the sense of being apart from the manifestation, of it being 'out there' and me not being part of it. This shift happened over a period of a few days during which it was as if the 'otherness' seemed to flood into me. It was as if something had opened up within and this 'otherness' just seeped in, until I was transparent or hollow, and full with it the same as everything else. It was almost physical the way it happened and I could sense this 'otherness' as it were filling out within me. Afterwards, when I looked at things, ordinary things like the jug, or the window frame, there was a sense of being the same as them. I felt that I was a kind of empty appearance the same as they were. I was no more a real person than the window frame was a real window frame. It was all actually a manifestation of something quite 'other' and there was no real difference anywhere.

Conflict and Pitfalls

This description of how things were after January can make it sound as if I was living in an experience of unitary oneness but that is not at all how it was. It is simply that through this shift the sense of being apart from the oneness-being-everything, which before had seemed to embrace everything else but not include me, disappeared fundamentally. It is very easy to write, and talk, however as if these things are black and white, when they are not. After what happened in January there was not the complete living of oneness in some way, but rather on some level that I do not pretend to understand, there was now a clear sense that I was the same as everything else, that we were all the same reality without any real separation or apartness. That did not, however, preclude the sense of personhood still coming back again afterwards. The moving back and forth between

144

experiencing things as a 'person' and experiencing them impersonally continued to carry on. And in some ways, it was now accentuated. During the time after Wales, but before January, nothing very much had really changed on a personal and experiential level. There was the sense of being home and of seeking being over after decades of feeling separate and cast out. And the sense of everything as wondrous had continued gradually to widen and fill out. But apart from that things remained basically the same as they had been after I had returned from Wales and I had no reason to think that they would ever really change. Now, after January, I became aware that this was a process, that what had happened in Wales was not the end, but perhaps only the beginning of the end and that there was potentially a long way to go, with lots of shifts or 'stages' to go through. I began to understand more deeply what people meant when they talked about the 'crumbling of the personality or character' and that this took a long time, potentially years to happen.

During this time, the fact that the 'person' Nigel Wentworth came back made it clear that it was not 'all over' and that instead there was a long apparent process ahead through which all this would fill out and deepen. The impulse that then arose was to want it all over immediately or as soon as possible. I could see that that was just another expression of self-seeking as was the other desire to speed up the process. I could see that I had done nothing to make the shift that occurred in January happen; it had simply been the next step on a journey that had apparently been going on for a long time. It was also clear to me by now that anything that 'I' did was only ever an expression of self-seeking and only strengthened the sense of being a 'person'. But the simple knowledge that what was going on was an on-going process seemed to change things. I found myself wanting it to deepen and was impatient with things being the way they were. This did not take away the sense of having come home after Wales. That was still there and so I did not feel that I had gone back to seeking. Moreover, the experience of everything as the kingdom of heaven was there everyday. But, and in part precisely because of all these things, I began to feel frustrated with my continued tendency to re-identify with the 'person' and start behaving as if it was real. Part of my frustration was to do with the precise things that I did, when I acted from the place of identifying as a 'person', and some of it was to do with the simple fact that it happened at all. When I acted from that place, I would get annoyed, impatient and angry, I would judge people, believing that my opinions were true and my values right. Then, when those feelings were passed, all of that would look so absurd and new feelings would arise, of embarrassment that I could have acted in that way. But something else was seeing all of this, the identification, anger and irritation that came out of the sense of being a 'person', as well as the pain to my persona that this then created, and it was also seeing the delusional nonsense of it all. It made me feel like something of a charlatan, in that I was professing to myself and a few others to be a certain way, to see things and live things from a more impersonal perspective, and yet I could still go around behaving like the most ignorant, self-identified 'person'.

I knew, intellectually, that it was ultimately all the same thing. It was all oneness manifesting as whatever it happened to be, whether that was the wondrousness and love that ordinary things evinced, or whether it was me going around acting as if 'I' was a real person experiencing what happened to me as if it mattered and as if my beliefs about things were really true. Knowing this, however, did not make it feel alright. Rather, the more it went on the more unbearable it became. This was accentuated because the more time that passed the more what had opened up in Wales seemed to deepen and therefore the contrast with what arose when the sense of being a 'person' returned only became more acute. But also, more fundamentally, the two modes of being, that of a 'person' and that of impersonal beingness, are so different and so opposed, that to exist in both at the same time is uncomfortable to the point of being painful. Everything in the behaviour of a 'person' is the denial of everything that is seen from the perspective of impersonal beingness. From the latter perspective it is clear that all the assumptions that underpin the behaviour of the 'person' are not true. And we have a natural aversion to living in untruth. So, the same apparent body-organism cannot contain both within itself without feeling conflicted.

This sense of conflict that arose after returning from Wales due to the to-ing and fro-ing between the sense of being a 'person' and a more impersonal way of being over time led me to fall into various pitfalls that I think are quite common after awakening. The root of it all was that I became impatient for the process of waking up which seemed to have started after the weekend at Pax Lodge to complete. I found myself wanting it to be all over and for the sense of a 'person' to go once and for all. And, though I was not aware of it at the time, this led to forms of seeking resurrecting themselves.

The main form this took, for me, was trying to stay attuned to the sense of oneness as everything. Each day, and at any moment, if I looked at anything, even the most apparently mundane thing, it would appear as the incarnation of a kind of otherworldly presence, soft and still, and I would be lost in wonder. Each day it was there, apparently spread out before me, like the kingdom of heaven. And the more time passed, and the more I found the to-ing and fro-ing back in and out of experiencing myself as a 'person' unbearable, the more I found myself trying to stay with this experience. At some point I had the thought that if I could remain in this place, continually open to the kingdom of heaven, then I would no longer find myself falling back into experiencing myself as a 'person'. So, I started making the effort to stay in this place and if I noticed that I had lost touch with it I would try to get back to it. Now, when I look back at it, the ridiculousness of it makes me laugh, but at the time I was taken in by it. I felt myself to be in a kind of limbo, between two quite different and opposed modes of being and of shuttling backwards and forwards between them randomly. The way I behaved when I was 'me' again made me cringe and so I tried to stop it from happening.

Part of what underpinned this and drove it forward was a belief that the 'me' was fake and that only how I was and how everything appeared when 'I' was not there was real. Therefore, in order for me to live in reality all the time the sense of 'me' had to die and I had to wake up completely. As I understood it at the time, this would mean dwelling permanently in this experience of wonder. I was aware that however much I tried I could not just make this happen so, as well as trying to stay in this place, I also thought about trying to do something on a deeper level, to address whatever it was that made

147

me go back into the experience of a person. So, I set about reading a number of books by teachers of non-dualism other than Tony, people who include within their teaching some prescription or another as to how awakening is to be achieved. I found their ideas seductive as they chimed with my sense of how awakening had happened in the first place. In part, it seemed clear that it had happened through the seeing through of the structures of the personal identity that I used to think that I was. So, I came to think, if I learned to see through this to an even greater extent, then maybe that would help this process to move along. It all seemed very convincing and I tried one or two things, at least for a short time. But it never lasted very long at all, for the same reason that 'spiritual' seeking had never seemed possible for me, that it just felt like self-seeking, like me trying to get something for myself, which had always been the problem in the first place.

I could see all of this, at least to a limited extent, but not enough completely to see through it. It is only now, much later, that it seems clear. At the time, I think I was thrown by the magnitude of what had opened up in Wales and confused by the radically different and contradictory impulses and thoughts that were arising within me at the same time, and I simply got lost. I failed to see that the whole structure of seeking had simply started up again: the sense that whatever was going on was not 'it' and that there was a different 'better' alternative. In other words, the sense of being a 'person' had returned and with it that way of experiencing everything and engaging in the world. The way I was thinking presented itself as coming from the place of impersonal experience that had opened up after Wales, when in fact it came directly from the 'personal' space that is the experience of a 'person'. It was all about how 'I' could make things better for 'myself'. It took a long time for me to see it, but it was a perfect example of the way in which the 'person' can co-opt what arises out of awakening and turn it into a new identity. The way this can work is something like what follows: instead of 'my' sense of 'myself' being that of a normal person with a normal life, 'I' come to see 'myself' as an awakened person, with an awakened consciousness or experience. From the way 'I' see 'myself' changing 'I' come to believe that this consciousness or experience is not complete, that there is still some unawakened stuff going on, which leads to the further belief that something still needs to happen in order for it to complete. This then becomes 'my' job, to try to find a way to complete this process. And so 'I' set about doing 'this' or trying not to do 'that'. Ironically, and inevitably, this endless movement into the future, this return to becoming, sustains the very sense of being a 'person' that 'I' am supposedly trying to overcome. For the 'person' is becoming, the 'person' is the movement from 'here', which is experienced as not-good-enough, to 'there', which will be 'better'. The attempt, therefore, to complete the process of awakening by staying in an awakened space, however that awakened place is experienced, is the surest sign that falling asleep again has already taken place and the 'person' is back in control.

What is not seen from this point of view is that this whole way of thinking is entirely back in a 'personal' perspective, that is to say, one that takes the 'person' to be real. It starts from the belief that awakening has not completely happened, because the experience of going back into the 'person' still happens and it treats that experience as real. Actually, there never was a 'person' it only ever was a delusion to think that there was. So, going back into the 'person' is not something that ever actually happens, for there is no 'person' to go back into. It is only in the delusional experience of a 'person' that it can be believed to happen. Really, whatever arises is only the same unitary divine manifestation, including what is experienced by a 'person' to be that 'person' doing something. Actually, nobody ever did anything and nobody is doing anything and nobody ever will do anything. So, the whole experience of going back into a personhood is only ever a delusion. Therefore, there is no real to-ing and fro-ing between the experience of a 'person' and the impersonal experience of oneness being everything. Really, there is only something utterly impersonal manifesting as both.

The fact that this was not seen at the time was simply an expression of how much of the held-sense of being a person was still there. What it also revealed, however, was how effective that held-sense is at sustaining itself. It always manifests as a form of identity, but the particular nature of that identity is not important. One identity can be dropped and another taken up, without it hardly even being noticed. So long as there is an identity, however, whatever the particular nature of that identity, the held-sense of being a person can maintain itself, and that is all that it is trying to do. Therefore, the identity of being a spiritual seeker, on a spiritual path to awakening, is just as effective for the held-sense of a person to keep itself going, as the identity of being a successful person in the world, with a good job and a family, or any other form of identity. It really does not matter. The held-sense of being a person will co-opt whatever comes along and turn it into a form of identity that makes its continuance possible.

This was one pitfall that I fell into in the months after the retreat in Wales. Another one arises from a quite opposite reaction to awakening. This has as its starting point the realisation that actually there is no real person and that everything that occurs simply happens and is not done by anybody, as an expression of an underlying unity or oneness. This can be called the impersonal perspective. It is the seeing that no one works, or cooks, rather working or cooking happen. The seeing of the impersonal perspective can lead to a quite different strategy for the sense of a person to ensure its own survival thereafter. This strategy is for the self to say to itself that whatever arises is just an impersonal happening and therefore it is all the same thing whatever it is. Therefore, so it tells itself, it does not matter if there seems to be a return into the experience of a 'person', because there is no real person. Really no one does anything, so the fact that one seems to be behaving from a 'personal' place is irrelevant. This way of thinking provides perfect cover for the sense of a person to survive and with it the constructed identity that gives form to it. Action can continue to arise from that place, protected by the mantra that 'it is all one anyway, so it does not matter'.

So, for instance, someone can continue to try to satisfy his desires through an identification with them that is through and through 'personal'. What that means is that for him the satisfaction of his desires really matters because he still believes that it will lead to a state of affairs that is really better than how it would be if they were not satisfied. However, he does not see that this is what is going on, explaining it away as something that is simply happening impersonally. Similarly, someone can continue to react to people or situations 'personally', for instance through taking 'personal' offence, feeling 'personally' insulted or challenged, again explaining it away to themselves as an 'impersonal happening'. All of these things start arising again because the impersonal reality, that there is no person, is no longer being seen. Perhaps at one time it was, but the sense of personhood has come back and now there is only an intellectual affirmation of it. The result is that it is not being lived, for if it is really seen and lived that there is no personal self then there will be nobody to have a 'personal' reaction and no energy behind attempts to try to satisfy a 'personal' desire for something, because there will be no sense of there being anybody for whom it would be better either way whether they are satisfied or not. This strategy for the sense of a 'person' to survive was never as powerful for me as the previous one, but there were times, particularly after I had sometimes behaved in ways that I was not proud of, when I found myself using this as an excuse to myself.

This perspective, however, does have some truth in it, just as did the previous perspective that the process that began after Wales did not seem to be complete, because the experience of a 'person' kept on returning. Both perspectives are a partial truth, one that can only be seen aright from a wider perspective that takes in both. So, it was true that what seemed to have opened up after Wales had not completed, because the sense of being a person kept on returning. But that was only a partial truth because it was also true that that sense of being a person was only ever a delusion anyway, and therefore any movement to try to do something to hasten the end to the process of crumbling is only an expression of a return to the very delusion it purports to be trying to bring to an end. And in relation to the second pitfall it is true that there is no real person who is separate or apart and has free will and choice to decide how to live 'their' life. Therefore, if someone seems to have 'personal' reactions those reactions do not really come from a personal place because there is none. But that is only a partial perspective, because clearly the *sense* of being a real person has survived, since acting from that place continues to arise. Therefore, for someone to say 'there is no real person, so nobody really does anything and so it does not matter what is done', and as a result to carry on acting from the place of a 'person', is for everything that was seen in awakening in effect to be forgotten. In short, both paths are an expression of the fact that the body-organism has gone back to sleep again; they are both an indication that the held-sense of being a real person has regained sway.

Part of what fuels and sustains this apparent going back into the 'person' is fear. The anticipation of the loss of the sense of being somebody is fearful to the self. Since the sense of being someone originally arose early on in life that is all the apparent body-organism has known. To a body-organism that experiences itself as a real 'person' the idea of all that makes it up disintegrating is deeply frightening. When all there has ever been is a sense of identity, whether as a man or a woman, a father or mother, a Christian or Muslim, an Englishman or a Frenchwoman, a manager or a worker, someone serious or someone light, a spiritual seeker or someone worldly or whatever it may be, the idea of not feeling that one is really any of that any more can be unnerving. From the place of a 'person' it is simply impossible to imagine living without an identity of that form and that breeds great fear and resistance towards anything that is experienced as a threat to it. The sense of self therefore tries to hold onto whatever arises within experience and turn it into a new identity as a way of maintaining itself. So if what is seen is that something of the sense of a 'person' has survived awakening this can easily turn into a new identity in the form of a path of becoming that needs to be followed and which 'one' will now follow until awakening is complete. Whether this new path and new identity forms around the belief that because 'one' is not fully awake what 'one' needs to do next is to try to get there and stay there, or whether it forms around the thought that because actually everything is oneness being that and so there is no real 'person' therefore it does not matter what happens because it is all one anyway, or any other form of identity, does not matter for the sense of self. The only important thing is to maintain a sense of identity as what 'I' am, inevitably in the form of a path of becoming that 'I' am on. The precise nature of that path and identity is by the way.

At various points after the retreat in Wales, this sense of fear as to where this process was leading was palpable within me. There were times when the realisation that the whole sense of identity that I had carried around for so many years was in the process of crumbling felt completely unproblematic, but there were also others that left me feeling quite anguished. The fear and anxiety were always in anticipation. After something had fallen away there was never any regret about it, or even a sense of loss. It was always as if nothing had really happened and certainly that nothing of significance had been lost. Whatever was gone no longer felt part of me and therefore the fact that it was gone simply did not matter. Beforehand, however, it was a different matter and the idea of something that still seemed to form part of my identity falling away did not feel at all comfortable. The critical word here is 'idea'. The fear only ever arose out of an idea of how it would be. It was just a construction of thought, the projection of an imagined future, which 'I' then reacted to. By contrast, whatever just *was* I always experienced as being perfect just the way it was, however much of my sense of identity had previously crumbled away. There has never been a moment when I have wished that some of the old sense of identity could return again. In the process of something going there has been sadness and a sense of loss, but that always disappeared quite quickly and then everything has always seemed perfectly whole again.

Jura

For quite a few months all of this carried on, the to-ing and fro-ing between experiencing myself as a 'person' and experiencing everything impersonally, as well as the attempt to stay with the experience of everything as the kingdom of heaven. The fact that both these things were going on made life feel quite conflicted. The to-ing and fro-ing between experiencing myself as a 'person' and not was something that just happened, but I was not comfortable with it and somewhere there was resistance to it. This resistance arose also as a result of the deepening of the experience of everything as the kingdom of heaven. To see things in that way brought a deep joy and some of the most intensely joyful moments of my life had occurred over those months, as the kingdom gradually widened and deepened, gradually becoming everything. Alongside the joy, however, I had also come to see that experience as somehow 'better' than ordinary experience of the apparent world. And so, for both these reasons, I wanted to stay with this experience and resisted leaving it, and that gave rise to conflict.

Both of these sources of conflict resolved themselves, or at least began to resolve themselves, the next summer after the retreat in Wales when I went to the Isle of Jura for a week. While I was there, two things happened which together seemed to unlock the knots that gave rise to this conflict. The first was that I became aware of the extent to which I had carried with me a deep sense of personal unworthiness for as long as I could remember and that this had, directly or indirectly, fuelled so much of my experience of life. I had never really thought about the sense of worthiness or unworthiness before. It was something I had heard Tony occasionally speak about, but it had never really resonated and up to this point had not seemed significant. I now became aware that it was not only significant it was one of the major drivers of the whole structure of personal becoming. This gradually emerged the more I thought about our sense of self-worth, and in particular 'my' sense of self-worth, how it has come into being, what underpins and sustains it and the effect that has on the way life is experienced and lived.

What I came to see was that all of our conditioning, really the whole of our conditioning, teaches us that we are not good enough as we are. In essence that is what our conditioning from our parents and our schooling and society teaches us. It can manifest in different people in different ways, but the core of it is always the same; we learn through the conditioning that we are not alright as we are and need to become 'better', in some way, however that is understood, whether in the form of becoming 'better' internally by changing the way we are, or externally by getting to a 'better' place. This all starts very early on in life, in effect from when the first person praises us for being 'good' or criticises us for being 'bad'. We start to learn that we are not really loved or valued for how we actually are, but in large part for how we match up to other people's expectations of us. We learn that how much we get of what we really need and yearn for in life, love, care, respect, support and protection, depends on how other people perceive and experience us; in short, whether they find us 'good' enough. What this creates is a conditional sense of self-worth, one that becomes a cornerstone of the whole identity that is the 'person'. This conditional sense of self-worth then fills out into the particular identity that we eventually come to have. We learn that we will only get the love that we need from our parents *if* we behave in the right way, that we will only get the praise that we need at school *if* we do well enough, that we will only have the friends we want *if* we conform and that we will only succeed in life *if* we work hard enough or are intelligent or pretty enough. Whatever we do and whatever place we come to have in society is based on a sense of conditional worth in relation to that. And this in turn is grounded on the nature of those values within the particular society we live in. So, for instance, if my sense of identity is based on 'me' being successful, what that means depends on society's criteria of success. I cannot define myself as 'successful' if society does not agree with my definition. Other people would simply see me as deluded. So, to be really 'successful' I have to conform to society's criteria, and these criteria are entirely relative. In a modern Western society to be 'successful' might be defined in terms of having wealth greater than x, or status higher than y. But these are relative terms, 'greater than' and 'higher than' and it is the same with all the criteria that give form to the identity of a 'person'. Whether a person's identity is based on how successful, or intelligent, or pretty, or hard-working, or devout, or serious, or funny they are, or whatever it is based on, it will only be a relative worth, relative to other people's views in this respect. That is to say, it depends on what is considered normal, what is considered poor or low and what is considered good or high, in respect of that quality within that society. An identity founded on these criteria has, then, only a relative worth, relative to the criteria of the society in which the identity is constructed. And it is also, by the same process, entirely conditional and dependent on the views of other members of that society.

Thus, as our sense of ourselves as a 'person' develops through life, that is a 'person' with a particular identity, we come to experience ourselves, even if we are not aware of it, as having an entirely conditional and relative self-worth. And this in turn creates within us a deep sense of inadequacy and unworthiness. This arises because a relative and conditional self-identity is intrinsically insecure. Whether 'my' identity is based on 'me' being successful or intelligent, devout, or funny these are all relative qualities in a further second way. Some other people will invariably be more successful, or intelligent, or devout, or funny than 'me' and others will probably be less. That will give me a certain status, relative to these other people, but only relative to them. Obviously, in any respect, 'I' could be 'better' than I am. 'I' could be more 'successful', more 'intelligent' or 'prettier'. Furthermore, however 'I' am in any respect at a particular time can change. Circumstances could change in my life, or the lives of other people, causing my status to fall. I could become less 'successful', either by something happening to 'me', or other people 'I' know becoming more 'successful', thereby changing my relative position. The same thing could happen in relation to any other aspect of 'my' identity. 'My' status and therefore my identity is precarious and is only ever in a process of being created and recreated through what happens and the way 'I' and others behave. Secondly, unless 'I' continue to behave in a way that conforms to society's criteria, in whatever way that is, the approval from society that underpins my identity will be withdrawn. 'My' identity, then, is entirely conditional. It is not something that 'I' have within myself, it is something bestowed on 'me' by others. In a sense, what 'I' become is a construct based on other people's perceptions and judgements of 'me'. 'I' am not a thing that just *is*, rather 'I' am a kind of artificial social construct that is only ever in a process of *becoming*.

This conditionality, relativity and artificiality becomes the 'person's self-identity as a particular 'person' in a particular society and at a particular time, and it is this that gives rise to the equally held-sense of personal unworthiness and inadequacy that a 'person' typically has. For, how can 'I' be really adequate as 'I' am if what that is, is an artificial construct based on, and therefore dependent upon, the attitudes and values that obtain in my society? The nature of human personal identity as a social construct naturally generates a sense of insecurity and inadequacy, and that equally naturally fills out as a sense of personal unworthiness. This goes on to give a concrete form to the sense of lack that arises from the held-sense of personal reality and apartness. It is not just an abstract sense of lack because 'I' am real and apart from everything, it becomes filled out in relation to my own personal sense of my own identity, as 'this' and 'not-that', and this brings with it a constant sense of insecurity, inadequacy and personal unworthiness.

These things are so deep and so enmeshed within the very structure of a 'person' that it is easy to see straight past them as if they are not there or, if they are seen, to accept them as 'normal'. They are tied so intrinsically to our sense of our own identity and that identity, more than anything else, seems to be what we are, for it is experienced as precisely 'us', that it can seem impossible for it to be other than it is. And that was how it was for me. Somehow, this sense of personal unworthiness, and the identity that grounded it, had survived the awakenings in Paris and Wales, as well as the partial crumbling or disintegration that had taken place over the previous year. Or possibly, it was only because of all of what had happened before that it was now possible for me to see it. What I means is that it was only on the basis of what had been seen in Wales, and the shifts that that had brought about, that the realisation had opened up and deepened that I was not really 'me', the constructed identity that I had lived with for so many years, but actually something entirely 'other', and it was only this in turn that made it possible for this identity to be seen clearly for what it was for the first time.

However it was, on Jura there came about a moment of clarity in which it was seen that something of this sense of personal unworthiness had survived right up to now and that this was in part what was fuelling the sense I had that I needed to be doing something, trying to do something, to get to a 'better' place where things would finally be alright. This was what was going on every day, with the attempt to stay attuned to the experience of everything as the kingdom of heaven. I was seeing being in that place as somehow 'better' than the experience of ordinary life, because being in that place involved an experience of oneness being everything, which ordinary experience did not. And I had persuaded myself that if I could only stay attuned to that experience all the time, then everything would finally be good enough. When I saw all of this it was suddenly completely clear that all of that was really only the expression of the held-sense that I was not good enough as I actually was and that I needed to be different somehow.

What also became clear to me was that this sense of myself as not being good enough went right back to when I first began to experience myself as apart from everything when I was fifteen. When I think about it I realise that it must have its roots much earlier than that, but I am not aware of it in my experience. What I am aware of is that from this time I began to experience myself as cast out and somehow utterly apart and alone, with the profound anguish that that brought on, and this had given rise to a belief that somehow I must have done something wrong, lost something, or made a mistake somewhere and that I needed therefore to do something else so as to get back to a place of belonging, to home. I had held on to this sense through all the intervening years and through everything that had happened. I had always felt that something was missing and that I needed to do something to get it back. Even waking up in Wales had not shifted this. There was still a sense that where I was, was not good enough and that I needed to do something to get to a place where it would be.

In this externalising of the situation I was only doing what all people do. We always think that the problem is 'out there' and that what is needed is more of 'this', or less of 'that'. We never see that the lack is actually within ourselves and that 'out there' nothing is lacking at all. We always think that if only we had more money, a more loving partner, a better job, or a nicer home, that somehow it would be alright. We do not see that it is only a sense of inner lack that gives rise to this felt-need and that no amount of change 'out there' will ever rectify a sense of lack that has actually nothing to do with any of it.

In this way, we all create the worlds that we live within. 'My world' is the expression of 'me'. To the extent that 'I' feel a sense of lack, 'my world' will be experienced as lacking. To the extent that 'I' feel inadequate, 'my world' will seem inadequate and 'I' will feel the need to try to change it. None of us just inhabits a world. Rather, we are all the creators of the worlds in which we live. But not seeing that, we think there is something wrong in our world and that it needs to be different in some way.

On Jura, I came to see something of the nature of this structure to personal identity and the intrinsic sense of unworthiness that comes with it. It became clear to me in a way that it had not before that what I was, was not Nigel Wentworth, with the identity that that 'person' carried around, but something entirely 'other'. This 'otherness' was not anything in particular, because ultimately it was everything. It was not white, or male, or English, it had nothing to do with painting, or parenthood or loving trees. It simply *was*, as a kind of constant, beneath all of that. These other attributes were just incidental, how my identity as a 'person' happened to have developed. What I really was, was absolute 'otherness', or the divine, which somehow manifested as everything, including what appeared as 'me'.

And with this came the realisation that the sense of personal inadequacy that I carried around, and which drove the whole structure of becoming, was to do with the personal identity of Nigel Wentworth. 'He' was not good enough and never had been. 'He' had always been trying to become good enough or get to a place that felt good enough. But it was also clear that because of the way that 'he' was constructed, 'he' never could. What 'he' craved, what 'he' was always seeking, was belonging or unconditional acceptance and that could never be found through a sense of conditional self-worth. It did not matter how 'well' 'he' did at painting, how 'good' a parent 'he' was, or whatever 'his' personal character was like, that was never going to gain 'him' the sense of unconditional belonging that was all that 'he' really craved, because they were all relative and conditional.

At the same time as seeing this, I also saw that my real nature was as that 'otherness' which is the divine, and that as 'that' nothing was needed because 'that' does not have a sense of conditional self-worth. 'That' is absolute 'otherness' manifesting as everything, in the eternal present. It is the beingness that is everything. Beingness needs no approval. It cannot be 'better' than it is, for it just *is*. It is not going anywhere, does not need anything and lacks nothing.

When I saw that this is what I really was, rather than the constructed identity that is 'Nigel Wentworth', something again seemed to burst or break. It was as if I had been caught in a spell for ever so many years and suddenly the spell was broken. This took a while to sink in, but there was an immediate shift that then gradually filled out over time. What was suddenly clear was that everything is 'that', not just all the particular things that appear to be, but everything as a kind of whole that embraces whatever is. With that it was also clear that therefore within the appearance nothing was more 'that' than anything else. So, the experience of the kingdom of heaven was not more 'that' than the experience of being an apparent person going about in the world living an ordinary life. It was all the same thing. Whatever was was 'that', whatever it was and however it seemed. So, there was nowhere 'better' to get to, because nowhere was more 'that' than anywhere else. Everything was the same thing, for it was all a kind of unitary whole that actually never changed, whatever the appearance to the contrary.

With the seeing of this the whole sense that 'I' would be alright 'if I did this', or 'became that', or 'got that' seemed to be dispelled. I saw that all of that was simply an expression of the sense that what I was, was a real 'person', Nigel Wentworth, who carried around within himself a conditional identity from which arose a sense of unworthiness. Out of this the sense of something constantly lacking had arisen. With the seeing through of this that now occurred the whole impulse to become gradually fell away. Once this sense of personal identity and unworthiness had been seen through, it was clear that what I really was, was an unchanging beingness that just was, however I was and whatever I did, and that therefore there was no need to try to change anything or get anywhere because whatever that would be there would still only ever be this same beingness.

And with that the whole movement of becoming began to slow down.

What I had always craved, and what had always fuelled the drive to become, was unconditional belonging, or love. And with this shift, this began to arise naturally. There is nothing conditional about beingness, or the sense of absolute 'otherness'. It just *is* and never goes and never changes. The seeing that I was that removed my sense of conditional worth and with that arose a sense of being unconditionally alright just as I was and with that there was a natural sense of well-being. This sense of being unconditionally alright just as I am manifests as the experience of being unconditionally loved. This arises naturally out of the experience of oneself as pure beingness, the incarnation of the 'otherness' that is the divine. Beingness in a way that cannot be understood is unconditional love and to experience oneself as part of that beingness, as just beingness, is to be unconditionally loved and loving. But precisely because it arises out of beingness, the very opposite of a 'person', it does not belong to anybody, nobody has it, or does it. It just is.

Ironically, once the whole machinery of becoming had started to come to a juddering halt, and the tendency to try to stay attuned to the kingdom of heaven gradually came to an end, the sense of oneness as everything, the experience of which had been the object of the seeking in the first place, now simply arose naturally, as it became clear that everything in the manifestation just was beingness and unconditional love.

The sense of personal inadequacy also began gradually to crumble away. A 'person' will always feel a sense of inadequacy because in experiencing himself as having a particular identity he will experience himself as limited and therefore of only relative and conditional worth. The realisation that what one really is, is not any of this, nothing particular or limited, is the beginning of the experience of limitless being. This limitless being is not anything in particular; it is not white or black, Western or Eastern, male or female, intelligent or stupid, attractive or ugly. It just *is* and can and does manifest as everything that appears to be. To realise that one is this limitless being is to realise that one is nothing in particular, for anything particular would be limited. And because it is not anything in particular it is not limited in any way. Therefore, there is no sense of there being anything wrong with it or of it needing to be different. For it just *is*. The sense of personal inadequacy, then, just falls away, for there is nothing particular or limited left to feel inadequate.

Furthermore, the more that the sense of limitless being opens out and deepens, the more the whole conditioning is seen through, as being just that, a form of conditioning. What makes up that conditioning is no longer experienced as what I really am, but as only what 'I' am, in my case the constructed personal identity that is the 'person' or character Nigel Wentworth. That does not mean that it just disappears. It does not. The character or identity remains; it is simply less and less identified with. There is a sense of being something entirely 'other' and with that the energy goes out of the character and the constructs that form it, for instance, the interests, values and beliefs or opinions. The constructs that form the character thus come to be seen as a kind of outer shell that is somehow still worn, but is not what one really is.

Emptiness

Coming to experience myself as limitless being did not involve simply the crumbling of aspects of the character, or constructed identity, but more fundamentally a gradual de-identification with the whole identity structure. The more the identification with the particular aspects of the character fractured, the more the whole structure came to be seen as simply an artificial construct that simply was not what I really was at all. That construct was, however, what I had always experienced myself to be. Therefore, the de-identification with it, that really opened out and deepened after Jura, eventually led to a more profound shift a few months later. What seemed to happen was that at that point the whole identity structure just seemed to separate off. It did not collapse or disappear, however, rather it remained, but now in the form of an external construct, as it were, out of which the energy or investment had simply gone. I continued to act in the ways I used to, but there was no longer the feeling that I was really doing it or invested in it. Instead it seemed to occur as a kind of exterior happening, but one I was not really involved in. Somehow, what I was, or what I sensed myself to be, was something apart from this constructed identity and the activity it gave rise to. What that was I did not know and at first it did not seem to be anything at all. This is what gave rise to the sense of emptiness. I no longer felt myself to be all the actions, thoughts and reactions of this body-organism, but nor did I feel myself to be anything else either. The result was just an experience of emptiness. The shell of the former person Nigel Wentworth remained, but with nothing in it any more. It was an odd experience and quite disjointed. I would still do things, say things, respond to things, but it no longer really felt like me doing it. It all just seemed to happen automatically, but I was somehow not invested in it any more. So, animation still carried on without the sense of an animator making any of it happen. This created a strange feeling of desolation, though it was more odd than anything else.

Over time I got used to things being this way and it came to feel normal. With this experience of empty hollowness also came a greater peace or calm. This seemed to arise because in the absence of the sense that I was really engaged in things and doing them the whole drama of life seemed to reduce enormously. It was like a second collapse, the first having happened in Wales. Then, aspects of my held sense of identity had seemed to collapse. I now realised, however, that the larger structure that they had been aspects of had not. In retrospect I think this was why I had felt so schizophrenic for a long time after returning from the retreat in Wales. In the shift that now occurred, it was not just aspects of my held sense of identity that seemed to collapse or separate off, as not being what I really was, but the whole underlying structure. This felt far more like the death of Nigel Wentworth than what occurred in Wales had been. It was not just bits of me that seemed to crumble or fall away this time, but rather the whole sense of me as any kind of a person seemed to split off leaving only a sense of hollowness or emptiness behind. Again, this was not all instantaneous. There was a marked shift over a period of a few days, but then later as time has gone on it has continued to deepen and fill out. And I can see it being endless.

What this process has left behind is something that feels like a kind of empty shell, a body-organism without a 'person' in it. This is not a complete blank. For a start, the natural characteristics of the organism remain. For instance, this organism happens to like green more than any other colour. It also likes chocolate but is not keen on liquorice or the taste of aniseed in general. Besides these natural characteristics there is the whole conditioning that the organism has been exposed to; all of which also remains, continuing to manifest as a particular form of feeling, thinking and behaving. These things carry on happening but are now increasingly experienced as a succession of things that seem simply to occur. They are, and are experienced more and more to be, quite impersonal. There is less and less sense of someone doing any of it. It all simply arises out of I know not where and for I know not what reason. In short it simply is. Functioning simply happens. It does not happen to anyone, or for anyone, nor is anyone doing any of it. There is no 'ghost in the machine', responsible for what happens. It simply happens. There is only a functioning machine that goes on and on feeling, thinking, acting. It is simply going on. And then, one day, it will stop, apparently. But in the meantime, it just goes on.

This shift can be understood as the deepening or filling out of the impersonal reality that had opened up after the retreat in Wales. It did not involve any deepening of the sense of everything as the expression of an underlying oneness, but simply the collapse of what can be called 'personal' being. With that the impersonal reality that there is no one came to be more fully lived than it had been before. And the way that manifested was as the living of the apparent functioning that arose as something that simply happened.

This sense of the body organism simply functioning comes in tandem with the absence of a sense of living in a story, or a collection of stories or narratives. Stories or narratives arise in thought as a construction upon what appears to be going on. In part they constitute the 'person' experiencing 'himself' as living in a drama the nature of which is framed by the content of the stories. They come to be experienced as real, as something that is really going on and the actual situation, which is that there never was a story and that nothing of that kind was ever really occurring, is lost sight of. With the onset of the sense of empty beingness this sense of living in a story and of that story feeling like a real drama, alive and vital, gradually weakened. Simultaneously, and by the same movement, the sense of living in time, in a movement from past to future, weakened too.

This weakening of the sense of living in a drama brought about with it a marked reduction in thinking in general. A lot of the time thought is a kind of commentary on what is happening, in which the 'person' voices their response to whatever it is, typically fantasising about how things 'could' be in the future or 'should' have been in the past. In the absence of a sense of life as a drama there is nothing to manage and therefore this kind of thinking largely falls away. That is not to say that I do not think any more, but I think a lot less than I used to. There is simply much less to think about.

What thoughts do arise also tend not to be responded to emotionally in the same way. The emotional response that we have to thoughts typically arises from our sense that things could be different from how they actually are. So, if someone behaves in a particular way, for instance selfishly, putting themselves before us, we tend to judge that and can get quite hot under the collar about it. We do this because we experience how they acted as something being done *to* us and we think that they 'could' or 'should' have acted other than the way they did. This response on our part is based on a held-belief that they are real 'people' with free will and choice and therefore we respond to them in a completely different way to the way we respond to other things than people. We do not have a sense that the way a tree is could be different from how it is, or a beetle, because we do not have a sense that these things have free will and choice. We accept that they just are. The more then that it is seen that human beings are no different from this, that they are just manifestations of the divine the same as everything else, and that there is no 'person' inside with free will and choice, the more the way they are is accepted in the same way as the way a beetle or a tree is. We do not think that a beetle 'should' be different from the way it actually is, and other people come to be seen in the same way. They just *are*. There is nobody making them the way they are and nor is there anybody who could choose to be different. The way they are is simply how it is. Therefore, however selfishly somebody might behave, it is seen that that is simply how it is and that it could not have been otherwise. And from here it is then seen that because nobody could act differently from how they do act, nobody ever actually acts 'badly' or 'wrongly', any more than a tree or a beetle does.

This realisation that people have no personal responsibility for their actions leads to a further realisation that they cannot reasonably be blamed and held to account for them. This comes to seem straightforwardly obvious because if nobody could act differently from how they do in fact act then they cannot be held responsible for what they do?

This does not mean that there is a passive acceptance of whatever other people do. It can be seen that they could not act differently from the way they do, but that does not mean that we like it and that we just lie down and accept it. Not liking it can still arise and therefore so can refusing to accept it. All that goes is the sense that there is someone who could or should have acted other than as they actually did.

That said, what arose from this in the few months after I began to feel the sense of emptiness was a different way of relating to people and situations. The best way of describing this would be to say that the things that people did or that happened started simply to slide by. Before, when someone did something, for instance something that I did not like, I would typically react to it in the form of pushing back. I did that in part because my experience of the situation was that the other person 'should' not have done what they did. Now, the emptier I felt the more I experienced whatever I did as mere functioning occurring and the same with what other people did. As mere functioning occurring it was clear that it could not be different from how it was. This led to me seeing that there was nothing in the behaviour of the other person to react to emotionally any more than there would be with a tree or a beetle and so the reaction largely stopped. The way this seemed to manifest typically was that when something happened that previously might have brought on a reaction there was the beginnings of a response, but then nothing more. A reaction seemed to start within me and then there was a kind of seeing somewhere that it did not need to happen, that there was no need or reason for a reaction of this or any other kind, and so it did not come out but just died away again. What this has led to is that things just appear to slide by. Where before I would have engaged with them, and either start pushing or pulling at them, now there seems to be simply a kind of seeing of them, without any reaction, and so they just slide by and are gone. Again, it is not always like this. Sometimes reactions still occur, but they seem to less and less and the range of things that no longer trigger a reaction seems gradually to widen.

In this process, what I also see is that the beginning of a reaction to something that seems to arise is always an expression of my past conditioning. Things that have been experienced for a long time as a real drama and therefore as really mattering have led to patterns of behaviour growing up over an equally long time which are by now completely habitual. These old patterns are still there, but the impulse behind them seems to be fading away. The more the sense of emptiness filled out the more these reactions came to seem to belong to someone who I no longer was. They had arisen in the past as a means by which the character Nigel Wentworth tried to protect himself and make his experience of life work as well as possible. Now that character only seemed like an empty shell that happened still to be there. The reactions to push and pull at the world that arose within it no longer seemed to mean very much or be worth engaging with. All that was left then was something like the imprint of the reaction, without real force behind it. It is like an echo or a trace. It is quite odd seeing this happen. It is like an old bit of 'me' coming up, but then just dropping away again, because there is no impulse or energy 'here' behind it, wanting to pick it up and run with it. So it just momentarily arises and then just falls away again.

With other things, there is no longer even the trace of a reaction, for instance around how aesthetically attractive or unattractive things are. I see the difference between things, but there is no longer any reaction to it, or even the trace of one. Instead, it is almost the opposite. Despite having done so myself for so long I now find it strange when people go on about these things as if they are really important. It is as if they are missing something, something enormous that is right in front of them, and it seems strange that they do not see it.

It is not just thinking and reacting that largely comes to an end with the loss of a sense of living in a story or drama. Other things wind down too, for instance, planning, ambition, projecting, brooding; anything in short that is tied in with the sense of being a 'person' with a life that has a direction or purpose. In the absence of that, what arises is simple *beingness* without any sense of direction to it. Life just happens, without a sense that it is really going anywhere. As a result, it feels quite still, even when things appear to be going on. This is not the stillness that results from meditation or any other spiritual practice. It is the natural stillness that arises in the absence of the held-sense of being a person who is always on the move *to* somewhere.

This shift, from experiencing myself as a 'person' who had a life that was going somewhere, to an experience of impersonal beingness with no direction to it, was a much greater shift than say stopping reading history books or liking to visit museums. It was not the end of 'this' or 'that' aspect of the character, but rather a kind of stilling of the whole structure of becoming through which the character had previously lived. The result was a sense of emptiness that only became deeper the more time passed.

At first, this emptiness was experienced as rather bleak, akin to a form of nothingness. The crumbling away of the sense of being somebody with a life brought with it a sense of loss. For a time it felt quite barren or bleak. The sense of life that had been there previously, which felt like my personal life unfolding, gave it a drama and colour that was now no longer there. Compared to that personal life impersonal being at first felt grey and cold. All there was, was a hollow feeling; calm, but colourless and empty. Over time, however, this has almost completely changed. Experiencing myself as a person, I had always felt separate from things and they had seemed separate from each other. Existence felt fractured and incomplete. The more the sense of being a 'person' seemed to evaporate, however, leaving only a sense of emptiness, the more any sense of anything really being apart from anything else seemed to disappear and that brought with it an extraordinary sense of wholeness or fullness. Everything now appeared to be one single, unitary manifestation, whole and complete, without any sense of lack or of something being missing or lost. To experience things in this way felt extraordinary, because I had got so used to things feeling separate and lacking, but it did not feel particularly wonderful. Instead, it felt quite ordinary. It was a simple experience of me, as it were, just being and of everything else also just being. It was strangely ordinary.

In the absence of the sense of life as a kind of drama or play in which I was the chief actor, the sense that everything had a kind of direction to it also gradually weakened. The sense of narrative or story is not experienced by a 'person' only in relation to himself, but also everything else too and it is this that gives rise to the sense of a continuous 'world' that is always the same. Without that, everything seems fresh and new as if it had not been seen before – because actually it has not – but with that also comes the experiencing of everything as not really going anywhere. There is a timeless quality about everything that gives it a strange presence. Over time this has changed the experience of everything as the kingdom of heaven. When this had first arisen, over a year earlier, after the weekend at Pax Lodge, it had been as something wondrous and special. It was quite different from how things appeared in 'normal' experience and had a kind of radiance about it. As such, it gave rise to strong feelings of joy and well-being. It had remained like this for as long as it remained apart from 'normal' experience and as something that I seemed to re-attune to each day. After coming back from Jura, where I saw more deeply than I had before that the manifestation was not something that was only there in some kind of 'special' experience, but rather precisely the opposite, that it was simply everything, the need to return to this experience of things as the kingdom of heaven gradually fell away. Whether things were seen as that or not they were still the manifestation. No movement was needed, because however things were they were always that. The result of this was a massive relaxation, one that gradually deepened, as the felt-need to get to a 'better' place evaporated. And ironically, what that left behind was the realisation and lived-experience of everything as being the kingdom. It was no longer what was seen within a 'special' form of experience, different from 'ordinary' experience. Rather, it gradually became everything.

The Exterior Self

Emptiness is not nothingness. After the seeming collapse that occurred after coming back from Jura there was not 'nothing left' or 'nobody there any more', but rather a sense of emptiness. Emptiness implies something that is empty. And that was how it felt. I was empty, though in a rather peculiar way. In some sense I continued to be there, but only as a kind of empty shell. The best way that I can describe this empty shell is that it feels like an exterior self that is no longer who I really am.[11]   In a way, it can be understood as what is eventually left of the person-structure after awakening.

The 'person' is the construction that arises out of the interplay between the apparent organism with its innate make up and the conditioning that it experiences through life. The innate make up of the apparent organism being innate does not go. Sensations, percepts, thoughts and feelings continue to arise and therefore life continues to play out in the phenomenal world that arises through them.

---

[11]The notions of the 'inner' and 'outer' or 'exterior' self are traditional Christian ideas and go back through St Augustine to Paul. In traditional Christianity by the 'exterior self' is meant something similar to what in this book has been called the 'person'.

Moreover, the conditioning the apparent organism has been subject to throughout life does not disappear after awakening and therefore neither does the construct that has developed through it. In my case, some of what had developed through my conditioning seemed to just collapse after awakening leaving no trace, for instance the desire to paint and an investment in aesthetic discrimination and value, but many other things seemed to survive, for instance the Left-ish political opinions that have developed gradually through my life. Over time, however, there has been a gradual but constant crumbling of those things that survived the initial collapse after awakening. Every so often I notice that something more that used to be there no longer is. But something remains and my sense is that something of it always will. The form of beingness that has arisen through all these years of conditioning will never completely fall away.

So, there seems to be a thinning out or crumbling of the exterior self that takes place gradually over time after awakening. It is sometimes said that after awakening there is no one there any more and that how the apparent person continues to act is simply the expression of the innate make up of the apparent organism. It is this thinning out or crumbling away of the exterior self that makes it clear that this is not accurate. The way the apparent organism behaves is not just an expression of an innate make up, for if it were it would remain constant; it would not gradually crumble away over time. But this is precisely what happens.

Even things that appear quite fundamental, such as my sense of being English, have seemed to weaken or mutate. In other ways, however, the exterior self seems ineliminable. After awakening, life continues to be lived out in the relative, or phenomenal, world. We continue to live in a home, to work, pay tax, perhaps drive a car, have holidays, go to the cinema and shop. And we continue to act out the roles that go with these and other activities. We also continue to behave appropriately in public, greet people who we know with different degrees of familiarity and in general conform to the social conventions that make up the society we live in. All of these things involve what can be understood as our exterior self. And something of this will always survive, so long as we continue to live and function as a human being.

This does not mean that there is always the sense of being a 'person'. The 'person' is an exterior self that is held to be, or experienced to be, real. Awakening dispels the sense that this self is what one really is, but it does not thereby take away the existence of everything that constituted the structures of that self.

I have said that aspects of the exterior self seem ineliminable because they are required for functioning in the relative world to take place. Of course, functioning in the world does not need to take place to any great extent, but equally evidently no one can choose whether or not to do this. Were disengagement from the relative world to arise naturally, to that same extent would the exterior self diminish. That does not mean that the less of the exterior self there is left the better. The exterior self is as much an expression of the divine as its absence. There is nothing 'better' about a body-organism in which there is little remaining of the exterior self than one in which there is more. To believe that there is, is to be back within a dualistic perspective, according to which things are real and exist apart from each other and some of these things are really better than others. All of that is delusion. Nor is the above an encouragement to someone to try to disengage from the world in order to lessen the exterior self. Any attempt to do this would only be the expression of the very exterior self that it is purporting to weaken. So far from weakening it, then, it would only in fact have the opposite effect of reinforcing it, only in a different form.

Something of the exterior self, then, will always survive after awakening. How much depends on how much light entered the organism at the time of awakening and how far the process of the crumbling of the exterior self has gone on as a result. There is, however no significance at all as to how far this has actually occurred. If more light enters the system there will tend to be less engagement with what remains of the exterior self and so it will tend to wither or crumble. If, on the other hand, less light enters the system more of the exterior self will tend to survive and this will manifest as a greater continued engagement in the forms of life and conventions that make up that person's society.

Being the result of the interplay between the innate make up and conditioning the exterior self is entirely accidental. As such, it could not be less our true nature. It is something that just happens to arise, in whatever form that takes. I did not choose my innate make up, or the conditioning that I have undergone. And, therefore, to no more of an extent have I chosen my exterior self, for that is only the outcome of the interplay of these two factors. Whatever arises out of them are merely accidental characteristics that just happen to arise. They are completely impersonal and could not be less 'personal'; though to the 'person' who identifies with them and sees them as 'his' very nature they could not feel more personal.

Once these characteristics of the 'person' are seen through for what they are, as merely accidental forms that result from conditioning, they are no longer experienced as what one really is. The expression of them therefore feels more like the acting of a part in a play that one has not chosen than the living of one's life, which is how it used to feel. It is like wearing clothes that no longer fit but have become a size or two too big or small.

To whatever extent the exterior self survives awakening to that same extent will things continue to seem to matter. From a completely impersonal perspective, the perspective of the divine, everything is seen to be the same thing. Nothing is really different from anything else and therefore nothing is really better than anything else and therefore nothing is experienced really to matter. This is what is seen when the aperture is completely open, for however long that lasts. But at some point it closes again, at least to some extent, and needs to for functioning to be possible. Someone who remained in a place of constant openness to the divine reality would cease to function and probably not live very long. This return to functioning is therefore necessary. It is a return to life in the relative world, which is the world of the exterior self and it brings with it a return to the sense of things as seeming to matter. In this way, relative life carries on, however it does, after awakening. Of course, some things are only the expression of natural preferences, for instance for tea rather than coffee, but typically life after awakening involves a lot more than merely preferring tea to coffee. There is a regular engagement to bring about this end rather than that one, to make things this way rather than that. It might be seen that none of it 'really' matters – one is not back in the enthralment of the 'person' that one's personal story is real and really matters – but one still carries on doing it. For instance, after awakening people can continue to go on holiday. That is not a basic need, or even a natural preference. It is rather a kind of lifestyle choice. And the question that can be asked is: 'who cares?' or 'who wants, or needs, to go on holiday?' or 'to whom does it matter whether going on holiday happens or not?' The answer is the exterior self. To the extent that going on holiday still seems to matter, to that same extent is there still some sense left of a self, for it is precisely this self that has the desire to go on holiday and invests energy to bring it about. If there was the absence of any sense of a self whether going on holiday happened or not would not seem to matter at all and therefore it simply would not happen. The same for all the other things that can continue to happen after awakening beyond natural preferences, without some sense of a self that is invested in them they would simply fall away. The self that still cares about such things and is still invested in them is the exterior self.

After awakening, then, without any sense of the exterior self all there would be is the lived-experience of 'what is', whatever that happens to be, as perfect or complete just as it is. There would no longer be a sense of personal separation, and so no longer a sense of anything being apart and therefore of anything being lacking. Therefore, the basic desire for such a thing as a holiday even to happen would not arise, for such a desire implies some sense that it would be nice to have a break and that is to say that it would be better to have a break than not. Clearly, both of these only arise when there is some sense of self present, a self that has experiences some of which are experienced to be 'better' and others that are experienced to be 'worse'. In an experience arising out of the reality that there is only oneness appearing as everything there would be no sense that it would be better to go on holiday rather than not because there would be no sense of anything being apart from anything else that, or who, could go on holiday. Instead, there would only be an undifferentiated wholeness within which everything would always be perfect. Whether going on holiday happened or not would appear completely without significance because 'what is' would appear identical in the two cases. As a result, the desire to go on holiday would not arise and so going on holiday would not happen. Nor in fact would very much else. Functioning in the world would almost completely come to a stop. Even basic needs, like that for food, would not necessarily be satisfied because whether eating occurred or not 'what is' would appear to be the same underlying reality in either case.

This is rather extreme. But that is what the reality of completely impersonal being would be like. The complete living of the impersonal reality would mean the complete end or absence of personal need and therefore of desires arising to try to meet those needs. In practice, however, it is not what actually seems to happen. Something of the person-structure remains after awakening, to a greater or lesser extent, and therefore functioning in the world continues to that same extent. Of course, the 'person'-structure, or exterior self, is not a real self, for there is no separate self in any way. It is simply the remains of a *sense* of self-hood, of apartness and identity, one that seems to survive awakening. This sense is expressed in the patterns of behaviour that continue to arise out of whatever remains of the person-construct that has gradually built up since early life. So long as they continue to be identified with they remain. Over time, however, typically as the process that began in awakening deepens and fills out the identification with, or energetic investment in, what remains of this person-construct gradually weakens and with that the construct itself can gradually crumble away. Things that arise, for instance, thoughts, or feelings or desires that used to evoke an identified response no longer do so and instead they simply slide by. The result is a gradual thinning of the exterior self. This happens both through whole forms of activity that used to be engaged in just stopping, but also in the energy increasingly going out of those that remain. They carry on, for as long as they do, though without the sense any more of being constitutive of who one is.

This gradual crumbling eventually comes to be experienced as an enormous relief. There is freedom from the experienced-necessity of doing all sorts of things that the exterior self feels bound to maintain, for instance, being interested in things, having opinions about events in the world, caring about what happens, as well as having an investment in activities like going on holiday. These things form a kind of weight that we carry around with us, though generally we are so used to it that we do not notice it. It is only when one of them crumbles away or stops that the weight or pressure that it had formerly exerted is felt. This happened once when I was walking across the supermarket car park. It was suddenly clear to me in relation to an aspect of one of my children's behaviour that I had always reacted to in the past that it actually did not need a reaction or response of any kind. It could instead simply be left to slide by. The sense of relief and relaxation was palpable. It felt as if I had been carrying this rucksack on my back for so many years and somehow I had arrived at a place where I had just put it down and just walked on leaving it behind. There was an almost physical sense of lightness. And this kind of thing keeps on happening.

Interiority

After awakening, then, something of the person-structure survives in the form of what can be called an exterior self. That 'self' still pursues its purposes in the world, still tries to get things done, still discriminates between better and worse outcomes. But something different also arises after awakening. That is a seeing of everything as being equally alive, a seeing of 'what is' as something that is ultimately indescribable but which could inadequately be described as the manifestation of the divine. From this perspective there is no real separation anywhere and so no 'person', no separate self. All there is, is everything as a unitary manifestation, whole and indivisible and also unchanging. This unitary manifestation does not feel like the expression of nothingness. Rather there is the palpable presence of some *thing* manifesting as everything. This presence is the ground not just of everything else that appears to be, but also of everything that you and I appear to be and something within each of us knows itself to be that.

This something manifests experientially as a kind of interiority, one that can be sensed when the exterior self is still. The exterior self cannot make itself be still, because it only exists as movement and compulsion, but when it is still this interiority can be felt. I have earlier said that after the time on Jura the exterior self seemed to separate off leaving only a sense of emptiness behind, and that at first this felt quite bleak. This exterior self has subsisted, though no longer feeling to be who I really am. Alongside that, however, the sense of bleak emptiness that was there at first has gradually subsided as something else has seemed to fill out over time, something ultimately indescribable, but quite palpable. This is a sense of interiority in the form of what could inadequately be described as a form of impersonal presence or beingness. It is an impersonal presence because it is precisely not of 'me', Nigel Wentworth. Everything that was of him separated off as the exterior self. It was what was left behind, which had nothing to do with 'me', that I came to notice always had this same quality of presence or beingness. It is quite changeless, always the same.

That this beingness or presence had nothing to do with 'me', the identity Nigel Wentworth, can be seen from the fact that it is unchanging, whereas the identity of Nigel Wentworth has constantly changed over time. Nigel Wentworth used to be young, but is older now, he used to look a certain way, but now looks different, he used to hold various opinions about things, but now holds others. By contrast this beingness or presence has remained unchanged and unchanging. Whenever it is sensed it has exactly the same quality and I am aware that it always has been there the same as it is now. In a way, it has been the constant background to 'my' life as it has unfolded. Whatever has happened it has always been there, exactly the same. It was only because through life 'I' was always there, identified with my held-identity and the story that 'I' took to be 'my' life that I ignored and lost touch with it. But it is clear that it has always been here, timelessly the same.

As a form of beingness this interiority can be seen to be impersonal, unchanging and still. It just *is*, doing nothing, going nowhere. It also manifests, however, as a form of dispassionate awareness. It is dispassionate because it sees not with the eyes of a 'person', someone who is always grasping at what he sees, trying to possess it for himself in some way. Rather it simply sees, without reacting to what is seen. It does not grasp at things because it lives in the darkness of unknowing, knowing that it does not know, but also that what it seeks cannot be known. From here it is clearly seen that nothing really is what it appears to be, that the form of things is somehow empty or unreal and therefore there is nothing for it to grasp at.

As well as seeing the emptiness of form this dispassionate awareness also sees that these same forms are illuminated with the light of an unseen 'otherness', one which makes everything appear somehow both mysterious but at the same time also infinitely close. Seeing through the form of things it has no interest in them, the sort of interest that arises out of a knowing awareness, one that is always grasping at what it sees. There is thus a natural lessening of a tendency to push and pull at everything, either in a 'negative' form as annoyance, irritation and anger, but also as what are considered more 'positive' reactions, like interest and enthusiasm. As such, the form of seeing or awareness that manifests from the place of interiority can as well be described as 'disinterested' as 'dispassionate'. It has none of the interest in the world that leads us constantly to react to it. Instead, it sees with the eyes of dispassionate love, that same dispassionate love that emanates from everything when it is seen as the kingdom of heaven. That love is in us just as much as it is in everything else and is present in the simple awareness with which everything is seen when 'we' are not there. This dispassionate love arises naturally out of the same interiority that manifests equally as beingness, presence and dispassionate awareness. It sees everything as the same as itself, without separation or apartness, and has a natural love for it all.

Over time there has been a gradual deepening and filling out of this interiority in all its forms. It is more and more constantly there as my natural way of being and whenever it is a natural joy arises. This joy does not arise in relation to anything or for any particular reason rather it is just there. That is to say, it is the natural expression of this presence and dispassionate awareness and love that forms the interiority of us all. It is a natural joyfulness, expressing a deep sense of well-being that is ungrounded in, and unaffected by, whatever appears to be going on in life.

This presence and dispassionate awareness and the natural joy that comes with it is not 'mine'. It only arises when the 'person'-structure is still and as such it has nothing to do with 'me'. It is therefore not the expression of my true nature, for there is no me to have one. Rather it is the expression of the interiority that appears 'here', to the extent that it makes any sense to talk of 'here'. The nature of this interiority, which manifests as presence and joy as well as dispassionate awareness and love, is simply how the divine, that which is the ground and reality of everything, manifests in the human form when the 'person' is absent or still.

This interiority is always there. It is just normally dormant or overlooked in most people. From an early age they start to experience themselves as a separate 'person' and this sense of separateness fills out through life to form the full-blown adult 'person' structure. This 'person' is typically so completely given over to the exterior life, experiencing everything that arises as a drama happening *to* him, that there is no space for interiority, for the living of joyful, dispassionate beingness. The interiority, then, though always there in the background is generally not lived. This is true for some people to the extent that they are not even aware that it is there at all. But it is always there. It never goes. It is only 'we' who lose touch with it through our identification with ourselves as real and separate. Therefore, nothing needs to be done to 'find' it again, because it never went. And once it is found nothing needs to be done to abide in it for the same reason. Any striving to abide in a place of interiority is a sure sign that it has already been lost touch with. And any effort made to get it back again will only keep it away. Rather, when 'we' are absent it is always present as our natural way of being. Awakening, in part, is waking up to the existence of this interiority and the interior life that then over time gradually fills out. And it does only gradually fill out over time. It is not either there or not there, black or white. Rather it is dynamic, and gradually but inexorably deepens in the fullness of time.

As this sense of interiority fills out, it creates, as it were, a new centre that could be described as one of personal nothingness. In this place there is an absence of any sense of knowing this or being that, but also of needing this or that. Identification and desire consequently weaken leading to the falling away of the tendency to try to make things different from how they are. For in the place of personal nothingness it is seen that everything is already complete and so nothing needs to be different from how it is. It is from this place that things are let go of and allowed to slide by, because from here there is no need and so no agenda that would seek to direct things in one way or another.

Soon after awakening first happened in Wales, I have described how I had the sense that something had entered 'this' organism and was now gradually filling out through it. The image that always came to mind was of a drop of ink being dropped into a glass of clear water and then gradually dispersing through it over time. At first, the drop remains quite dense and concentrated in the centre of the glass. Gradually, however, it becomes more diffuse and fills out through the water until eventually the whole glass of water becomes a uniform colour. That image has recurred again and again and has always seemed the most accurate metaphor for describing the process that has seemed to be going on. Then, about a year and a half after the retreat in Wales, I read Thomas Merton's account of the nature of contemplative awakening and found that the term 'infusion' had been used over the centuries by Christian mystics to describe how awakening occurred. I had never heard the term 'infusion' before, but it seemed to describe exactly what I had been experiencing, that something had somehow entered 'this' organism and was gradually filling out through it.

The essence of the traditional Christian mystical understanding is that by the grace of God divine light somehow penetrates the darkness of the 'personal' soul bringing about an awakening that leads in time to contemplative union with the divine. This process has traditionally been understood to have various noteworthy features. The first is that it occurs entirely beyond personal will. There is absolutely nothing that the 'person' can do to bring about this infusion because it occurs in essence and by definition by the grace of the divine. Nothing that comes from the place of a 'person' can take one beyond the personal realm. Darkness cannot dispel darkness. Therefore, no amount of practice can ever bring on awakening. Rather, the investment in the very idea of practice, as a path that 'I' am on that will bring 'me' to awakening, only reinforces the held-sense of being a real person with a real life, which is supposedly the very thing one is trying to lose. However, if there is an openness or readiness, not as something that someone does but simply as an existent reality, then the divine light can enter the darkness, piercing the veil that somehow keeps us from seeing things as they really are.

The second feature of infusion within traditional Christianity is that it is of something, it is not of nothing. What results from it therefore is not nothingness, as a kind of blank that is left in the absence of a sense of the 'person', but rather the living of a sense of presence, the presence of that which has infused the apparent body-organism. When the sense of the 'personal' is absent or stilled there is not then a mere sense of everything as the expression of nothingness and of action arising out of that nothingness, but rather of some*thing* animating everything, including increasingly all that one is oneself. This is moreover the case because what enters and increasingly infuses the organism is of a quite different order of being to the 'personal' self that was previously present there. The more it fills out, then, the less is there the sense of 'personal' being and the more a sense of 'otherness' manifesting as impersonal, or what some writers call 'divine', being arising in its place. Being of a quite different order the 'personal' and impersonal/divine cannot occupy the same space. Therefore, there is also a gradual but inexorable process by which as the impersonal/divine fills out the 'personal' is reduced to the same extent. Finally, the fact that what enters the organism is of a quite different order to the 'personal' and that the two cannot co-exist together means that the more this sense of impersonal beingness fills out the more acting from a 'personal' place comes to be experienced as a kind of betrayal of all that is known to be true. There is therefore more and more resistance to acting from a 'personal' place and concomitantly a stronger pull to remain grounded in this sense of 'otherness' that is experienced to be the underlying nature of both oneself and everything else as well.

Being the nature both of ourselves as well as everything else, this light or 'otherness' that enters the organism is utterly impersonal. The more it fills out, then, the more the whole sense of 'personal' being diminishes. Ironically, so far from seeming like the end of oneself it feels quite the opposite, as if one is coming home to one's own most inward and truest nature. The 'personal' despite its name is actually entirely impersonal, for it is a construction that results in large part from the social conditioning that the organism has been subject to. This social conditioning is not an education of the organism to be itself, but completely the opposite, an indoctrination to conform to the expectations, norms and conventions of external society. What a person becomes is an expression of the supra-personal 'one'. A person learns how 'one' does this and that, that 'one' does or does not do these sorts of things and how 'one' behaves in particular situations. Acting as 'one' does and is expected to do is the very opposite of personal being. By contrast, the interiority that fills out through the process of divine infusion, despite having nothing of it that could be considered personal – for it is identical in nature to the interiority of everything and everyone else – feels like one's truest nature. To act from this place, then, feels like acting from a place that is home, whereas to act from the place of personal self-hood is to act from an alien place that has nothing to do with what one ultimately is.

Understood correctly, then, the nature of the process of infusion is actually the opposite of what it appears to be. Experientially it feels as if something has entered the organism from the outside. Actually, however, the divine always was the ground or beingness of all that we are. It always was that which manifested as everything that we appeared to be or do. It only appears that something infuses us from the outside because prior to the infusion there is an identification of oneself as a real person, with one's own personal nature, separate and apart from everything else. What has actually happened is that a crack has appeared in this false identity that has gradually widened, allowing something that was always there, but was somehow buried or hidden, to come to the fore. From the perspective of the person it feels like infusion from the outside, when actually it is only the loss of a false identity and a return to a natural beingness as that which one always already was.

Through this process that is the gradual shift from the exterior self to the living of interiority a paradox reveals itself. The more we act from the exterior self, or what remains of the person-structure, the more we actually only remain within the impersonal structures of social conditioning, doing what one has leant that 'one' does in this or that situation. We feel that we are being ourselves and leading our lives, when actually we are just acting out the roles that have been socially prescribed and delineated for us. By contrast, the more we come to act from the place of interiority, as the locus of an unknown 'otherness', the more we feel that we are becoming again what we have always most truly been, though how we are has nothing 'personal' about it. In short, we become aware that the 'me' is not me at all, while 'otherness' is what I have always really been.

The more this contrast becomes apparent between an unreal self that is the expression of social conditioning and an interiority that has nothing 'personal' about it but is our truest nature, the more I have said there arises a resistance to acting from a place of self, whether that be the 'person' who never really was or even the exterior self that seems to survive awakening. This resistance has been understood within traditional Christianity as the expression of the sense of sin. Sinfulness is conventionally misunderstood to arise out of the sense of having *done* wrong; but that is not it. To act wrongly is to transgress a socially constructed code and that gives rise to feelings of guilt. But, as Merton says[12], we can feel guilty for having done something that society forbids even if one does not believe it to be wrong oneself. The sense of sin arises not from what we have done, but from what we are. It arises out of the knowledge that I have gone against what I know within myself to be true, to be real, whatever anyone else might say. To be sinful then is ontological. It is to *be* wrong and to act against what one knows to be one's own truest nature, which is divine being.

This sense of sinfulness is the corollary after awakening of the resonance that was felt before. It is the expression of that within us which knows itself not to be the identity we have become and instead longs to come home, to dwell in unknowing, in silence and quiet, in stillness and in the love that are the nature of our inner beingness. For me, since returning from Jura after which the exterior self separated off, this sense of sinfulness became my regular companion to the same extent that I continued to live from the place of this exterior self. Something in me found it almost painful to play the game of a person, going along with all the conventional beliefs and expressions that I know to be ultimately hollow. In this sense, the apparent journey that is awakening is not just about whether the sense of being a real person is there or not. The loss of the 'person' is just a stepping stone. Once this has happened the real journey begins, which is the journey back to the divine, or God. Far beyond the psychological dropping of the sense of being a person this is an ontological shift back to an alignment with that which is the nature of everything. The sense of sin is that which keeps the interiority within each of us on its journey back to unity.

This journey feels like a return to something like honesty or plainness. It involves an apparent shift from being grounded in exterior form to living from a place of interiority. This gradually opens up through the deepening of the lived-awareness of everything, including oneself, as only a kind of manifestation of something quite 'other'. How things appear to be, then, becomes only an external

---

[12] Merton Thomas *The Inner Experience* Society for Promoting Christian Knowledge 2003 pp118-120

form, their real nature being that which animates them in that form. This has no knowable nature in itself and can only be experienced in the form in which it arises, but it is not so much that form as its ground. The form is only an appearance or manifestation, and so not real. That which is real is that which manifests in this form. What that gives rise to over time is an experience in which everything comes to appear to be hollow; mere form expressing an absolute 'otherness', one that is beyond sense and rational comprehension. That sense of the hollowness of everything takes in oneself. One becomes like everything else, absolute 'otherness' appearing in this form.

Thus, everything that appears to be appears equally not really to *be* at all, but only to be a kind of hollow manifesting of something quite 'other'. And it is in the contemplation of this paradoxical mystery that this interiority seems to abide. This mystery is constantly present in everything that appears to be, endlessly the same. To see it is to hear, as it were, a single note constantly being played through everything that appears to be, though it also somehow appears to be utterly silent at the same time. To see everything as the same thing is thus to be left in a place of contemplation or meditation on the apparentness of everything. This form of contemplation is calm and ordinary and arises naturally in the absence of a sense of direction or movement, when the exterior self falls still. It is like a contemplative, or unknowing, awareness. Within it, everything appears to have a constant freshness, or newness about it, even something that I only looked at a minute ago. It is as if everything is constantly being reborn and is alive with a sense of presence.

Just as the contemplative meditation on the mystery that is the beingness of everything arises out of the exterior self falling still so, in its turn, it removes the spur to action and movement that energises the exterior self. That spur to movement is born of the desire to get somewhere and make something happen, which itself arises from a felt-sense of lack. In the beingness of everything there is no lack and so nor is there in the contemplation of it. Inevitably, therefore, as the sense of interiority fills out the whole energy behind the exterior self just gradually and naturally winds down.

This also has an effect on personal relationships. In the absence of a sense of lack, people are no more experienced to be needed than anything else. That does not mean that there is a resistance to seeing people or engaging with them, more that there is simply a lessening of the felt-need to do so. So often in human life interaction with others is sought as a distraction from our own sense of lack, projected outwards and experienced as a lack in the situation we find ourselves in. Others become a distraction from our own sense of personal incompleteness. Inevitably, therefore, the more this 'personal' self crumbles, to be replaced by a sense of impersonal being that is limitless, the less need is felt for distraction or company. Communion, which takes the place of relationship, is felt as much in relation to the floorboards, or the sound of the fridge motor whirring, as with another human being.

This communion or communing is the interiority that we most truly are somehow seeing and recognising the same interiority in everything else that appears to be. In that recognition this shared interiority is sensed as a form of togetherness, belonging or unity. It is as if the interiority that I am is attuned to, or aligned with, the interiority that is everything else too, for they are the same thing. The living of that attunement or alignment is communion. This is not something that I do – obviously for it is a communion of being not of doing – it is rather simply the place that I seem endlessly to return to. And because this interiority manifests equally as everything that appears to be, because it is as much the floorboards as another human being, this communion is felt in exactly the same way with the floorboards as with another human being.

That communion is there as much with the floorboards as with other people does not mean that relating to other people somehow comes to an end. Relating carries on, in the sense of joining in the forms of behaviour that constitute the social expression of the person-structure. But all of that is of the exterior self. The more the sense of interiority fills out, the more we come to know ourselves to be the same divine expression as everything else that appears to be, the less is there any sense of there being anything apart, or separate, 'here' that could be in relationship to anything else. For how can something that knows itself to be the same as everything else somehow be in a relationship to it? Relationship requires two, and in a communion there are not two, but only one somehow seeming to be two. Communion, therefore, is something quite different to relationship; it is oneness in the form of twoness communing with itself, or the divine seeing and loving itself.

The complete end of a sense of 'personal' being would therefore bring with it the end of all felt-need for relationship. In practice that does not happen. The reduction in personal being does however affect how people are engaged with. Through the lessening of a sense of lack there is less sense of needing things *from* other people. In the absence of an agenda of what is wanted, or needed, from another person the struggle to try to get things from them reduces. This struggle characterises so much of the 'personal' relationships of a 'person', as he tries to ensure that his needs are met. These relationships tend to work so long as the 'person's' needs are met but fail once they cease to be. Even so-called loving relationships can sometimes boil down to this, the mutual looking after of two egos by two 'people' who experience themselves as separate and lacking. This looking after arises with the goal of achieving a kind of personal happiness for oneself and comes about through the recognition that this is much more likely to be achieved through co-operation and the mutual looking after of one's own and an other's personal identities.

This collapse of investment arises not just in relation to other people, but also towards the apparent world in general. What had once been experienced as the very real backdrop to a very real drama – my life – now appears to be somehow empty. A chair is not a real chair, a pear tree not a real pear tree. Instead, they are both the incarnation of something absolutely 'other'. Being an incarnation of absolute 'otherness', what they appear to be becomes just that, an appearance or manifestation, and as such empty. This drains away much of the interest and engagement with them in terms of their appearance. All that is left behind, then, is a contemplative wonder at the manifestation. That is not to say that life comes to an end.

Things carry on being done and things carry on being engaged with in terms of their apparent functions and how they enable us to fulfil our purposes, in part because they have to, at least some of the time, but the sense that it is all real and meaningful gradually goes. What is left in its place is simply the endless wonder at the simple fact of the manifestation. This single thing, that the divine appears as it does as everything is so extraordinary and so magical that once it has been seen the interest in the appearance largely fades away.

The more I came to see everything that appeared to be as the manifestation of something quite 'other' the more I came to experience that I was this too. With this gradual realisation there has come an equally gradual shift from a sense of emptiness in the form of a blank nothingness to a sense of fullness and presence, but just not as 'me'. There is the sense of something being 'here', it is just no longer experienced as 'me'. It could be described as a kind of impersonal energy because it is not tied to a sense of a personal drama. It is not going anywhere, has no agenda, but nor is it blank or bleak. Instead it has a fullness and warmth. In this sense it is not really impersonal at all, in the sense of there being nothing there. Something is there it is just not the identity of Nigel Wentworth. The more this has deepened and filled out the more it has felt like a homecoming. Gradually, I have come to realise that this interiority and the presence that is the divine in everything is the same reality. I can see that it has always been there just encrusted over by a false identity that was not really me. Over time, this has led to a kind of sinking back into a natural beingness that is both effortless and full of joy. When it is lived, which is whenever the exterior self is still, it feels entirely natural and obvious. Life continues to happen, but I am not living it. Instead it is effortless, like floating in water and being carried by the tide.

One way in which the filling out of the sense of being the divine presence has come to manifest 'here' is as a gentler and more accepting way of being. This has arisen gradually the more the living of interiority has filled out. The more it has done so the more the sense of personal unworthiness has fallen away, for there is less of anything 'personal' any more to feel unworthy about. In its place has arisen a natural love and desire to cherish 'this', the organism that I am and the life that goes on through it. Somehow, the emptying out of the sense of personal being and that emptiness being filled instead with a sense of fullness somehow brought a natural upsurge of loving acceptance.

With that has come a love, and cherishing, of everything else too. Outside of a sense of a drama going on, grounded on the sense that 'I' am here as a real 'person' with a real life, which leads to everything that is positive for oneself being experienced as 'good' and everything that is negative for oneself being experienced as 'bad', there is only a dispassionate acceptance of everything, however that affects oneself. Even things that other people had done to 'me' in the past that had caused 'me' pain and which had previously triggered negative feelings towards the people who had done them now appeared somehow neutral. I became aware that that in me which both is and knows itself to be the divine expression has never been touched by anything that happened to 'me', so that the more this interiority as the divine expression has filled out the more the personal hurts and resentments that in part formed 'me' are no longer felt and in their place there has just come into being a natural acceptance and peace. This shift, though marked, has not been complete. At times, the sense of being the 'person' Nigel Wentworth comes back and with that resentments can still arise. What I am pointing to is that now there is something quite 'other' there too, something that is not affected by what happens, or happened, in the flow. It is not experientially constant, and can still seem to come and go, but it has brought a quite different and much more loving experience towards whatever seems to arise within experience.

In a way, this can be understood as the arising of a quite different perspective from which everything is experienced. Before, everything was seen from 'my' perspective, which was parochial and limited. This gave rise to the rather petty sense of drama that used to fill it, in which everything was seen in accordance with how it affected 'me'. Now, the perspective seems to have taken on an impersonal and with that an almost limitless dimension. The same event can happen now as happened before, but whereas before it would be experienced as a personal drama, thereby giving rise to a personal response or reaction, now it arises against a completely different background that has a vastness about it. From this limitless perspective of everything as the manifestation of the divine however difficult or painful a particular situation might be from a personal perspective it still ultimately has a peace and stillness about it. Events that previously would have brought on an acute sense of personal drama and suffering now seem strangely alright, even though they can still be painful. It is as if everything, whatever it is, is somehow deeply perfect just as it is.

This timeless quality is present in the form or manifestation that is everything. Precisely because it is, however, both 'things' themselves as well as the changes they appear to undergo come to seem equally unreal. The apparent flux that is the world masks an underlying changelessness that is increasingly sensed. So, the cat continues to appear to move around on my lap, the trees outside still appear to rustle in the wind, but it is obvious that nothing is really changing. Somehow, there is a palpable changelessness or sameness that though it cannot be seen directly is somehow visible indirectly in everything that can be. This can sound mysterious, but to see it is to see something that is strangely obvious and straightforward, changelessness or constancy somehow appearing as all the change or flux that makes up the world for us.

Being supra-sensible and manifesting only in unknowing experience this unchanging presence cannot be described. This means that it cannot be shared or talked about. All normal talk inevitably, then, concerns only the form, not that which is present in and through the form. Worldly chatter is the very denial of this presence, through its identification of the form as real and so the locus of real drama. To relate on this level, to engage in conversation regarding the form of things and our interaction with them, is thereby to be drawn away from this presence and back into story and becoming. It is no surprise therefore that spiritual bodies have so often insisted on silence as a way of eliminating this pull back into worldliness. As well as being more accessible in silence than noise or chatter this presence is also experienced far more readily in solitude than in a crowd, or even with a single other person. And that further explains why people who have sought to live 'in God' have so often found themselves drawn to a life of solitude.

The sense of presence brings with it a feeling of gratitude for life. It is strange, but the more any sense of my 'personal' life has wound down the more this sense of a deep gratitude for the simple reality of life has filled out and deepened. So long as I felt myself to be a separate 'person' with a life that 'I' was leading this was never there. However 'well' things appeared to be going for 'me', there was always a deeper sense of dissatisfaction with life as a whole that never seemed to go. Now, though I have no sense that I am going anywhere in particular, or that my life – as it were, for there is really no me to have a life – has any particular meaning or significance, the simple living of it as whatever it is feels precious. Daily I am filled with gratitude for the simple experience of life and everything that appears within it.

To live in this presence is to live what Christian mystics called 'the will of God'. This is not the will of some being, for that is personal will. Personal will, or the experience of it for there is actually no such thing, is the will of a 'person', someone who wants things to be a certain way, in whatever way appears 'better' to him. It arises from the experience of the flow of life as a personal drama, something that is really happening to someone, to 'me', and therefore in which certain outcomes are experienced as better than others. As a result, to experience personal will is to be drawn inexorably into a pushing and pulling relationship with the world, resisting those outcomes that are experienced as 'worse' and trying to realise those that are experienced as 'better'. Central to that is the experience of different outcomes being possible in the same situation.   The experience of personal will, therefore, is based on the prior experience of oneself and others as having free will and choice and that is to say, on human beings being real people, separate and apart from the world and with free will and choice in the way they interact with it

The living of 'the will of God' is almost the precise opposite. It is not something that someone does, for everything that a 'person' does is the expression of what is experienced as personal will. Rather it is something that naturally arises once the self is still, the living of 'what is' as what it is and of not being capable of being otherwise. It is the living of the reality that everything that occurs just happens and that there are no 'people' with free will and choice doing anything, so nothing can be other than as it is. There only ever is 'what is' and it never could be different from how it is. To live aligned to 'what is' is thus to live that there are no different outcomes possible in the flow of life. There only is the flow, or the apparent flow, in which arises 'what is' as the one unitary reality. The more this is seen, the more there is an increasing evaporation of any impulse either to try to resist those outcomes in the apparent flow that are experienced as painful, or to bring about those that are experienced as pleasurable.

This living of the will of God does not mean to be acquiescent, or passive. That would still be to act from the place of a 'person', in this case from the belief that it is 'better' to accept things, and not resist them. Nor does it mean to withdraw from the world into a place of non-engagement like a monastery. That again would only arise out of a place where a 'person' is trying to make the flow 'work' for them, by separating themselves from the world so that they are no longer affected by it. To live as the expression of the divine is to live *in* the world, for the world is that expression too – that is precisely what it is – but just not *of* it, in the sense of treating what appears to go on within it as a real drama happening to oneself. It is the living of 'what is', as opposed to what 'could' or 'should' be. 'What is' is of the eternal present, eternal because there never is anything else, no future and no past. What 'could' or 'should' be is of the future, simply a projection or construction out of thought. Outside of the projections and constructions of thought, there is only the simple reality of 'what is' and the living of this is again very simple. When it is seen that nothing can be other than how it actually is, the tendency to push and pull at the world to try to make it as 'one' wants it to be simply falls away.

The more it is seen that everything just is the way that it is and could not be any other way the less is there a sense not just that it could, but also that it needs to, be different from how it is. As well as leading to the lessening of any attempt to try to control or direct the flow of events to make them meet our own personal needs, it also leads to a lessening of concern or worry about what happens. Whatever happens is in this way equally perfect and therefore the sense that it needs to be different from how it is, is just not there and therefore worrying about it does not arise. That takes the drama out of human life and also thereby the willingness to engage with it as if it were a drama. This kind of drama just does not seem interesting any more. Yes, the relative world still carries on and with it all the things that appear to go on within them. But they no longer feel like a drama that is really happening to anyone. Therefore, the interest in it all largely evaporates. This does not lead to a kind of callous indifference; if something needs to be done it is still done. But it does remove the energy to engage with events as if they are a real drama. This leads to an end to the kind of game playing that makes up so much of human relations; the engagement with the stories people tell themselves about their lives as if they are real and the consequent drama that thereby ensues. This does not mean there is a need to confront other people continually with this experience, but it does mean a lessening of a tendency to say things that one knows not to be true.

The loss of interest in the relative world is no more apparent than in the loss of interest in one's own life. The more this impersonal interiority fills out the less significance there seems to be in what remains of the exterior structures of the 'person'. The sense of being a person who *has* a life largely goes. The living of this feels like a great freedom. It is not the freedom that a 'person' imagines freedom to be, being able to do as one pleases. That is only a delusion and so far from being free the identification of freedom as that only leads to a kind of imprisonment. The self, believing that to be free it must be able to act as it pleases, is drawn into a constant struggle with the world to gain the freedom of action that it thinks it needs. It is a vain struggle, because that kind of freedom does not exist – not even the most powerful kings have ever had that kind of freedom – and the more it is struggled for the more enmeshed the self becomes in worldly conflict and strife and therefore the more imprisoned. Real freedom arises naturally and spontaneously out of living in the presence of the divine. The sense of 'personal' freedom is lost – but that was never real anyway – and in its place arises the much deeper and beautiful freedom of just being.

Absence

Eventually, nearly three years after this whole apparent process began over the weekend at Pax Lodge, there was another shift. This seemed to follow quite soon after the sense of interiority had filled out to the point where it was now more of a constant lived-reality. There was therefore now a more continuous living of the reality that all is actually one, without any real separation or distinction anywhere. The exterior self would still come and go, but there was now something else alongside or rather below it, the sense of being something quite 'other', which remained as a constant underneath all the exterior behaviour. This lived-sense of divine being, as the unitary reality behind all apparent phenomena, itself no longer came and went but instead formed the background against which everything else now seemed to occur. What this now seemed to lead to was a further deepening of what could be called the 'impersonal reality', that actually there are no real 'people' and that everything is just an impersonal happening.

This shift happened suddenly one evening and then as with others before it has gradually filled out through time. The nature of this shift cannot be described, however, because of the form that it took. This is because what changed was a further falling away of the sense of whatever appeared to be happening as something that was happening *to* me. And what that then left behind was simply whatever appeared to be happening, but not to anyone any more. This cannot be described because whenever we describe something what we are actually doing is really only describing an experience, how things appear to be for someone. So when there is no one, or no experiencer, there is no experience and therefore nothing that can be described.

One could attempt to describe it as something like the difference between me walking or sitting and there just being walking or sitting happening without a subject doing or experiencing it. But in the absence of a subject there is equally the absence of an object. What this means is that without an experiencer it is not just that there is no one for whom sitting or walking is happening, it is that what then is, is no longer graspable or describable, for instance as walking or sitting, at all. Talk of walking or sitting still involves 'what is' being grasped *as* 'this' or *as* 'that', in this case 'walking' or 'sitting'. And that is still a conceptualised story. Really in the absence of a locus of experience there is only an indescribable happening involving neither subject nor object. Being before both subject and object it is to the same extent and by the same movement before all conceptualisation, for it is in part through the very process of conceptualisation that the whole sense is created and maintained of there being a subject here experiencing an object there. Prior to that, prior to subject/object experience arising through conceptualisation and 'personal' identification, 'what is' is something ungraspable and therefore unsayable. This does not make it mysterious. It is not something strange or esoteric. It is simply 'what is' before it is conceptualised and turned into a personal experience. It is really very simple and ordinary; only it cannot be described.

When this happened, one effect was to change the way this whole apparent process appeared to me. The reason for this can perhaps best be explained in relation to all the apparent changes that had happened before, since this whole process began. At first, there had been the sense of wonder at the way everything seemed to radiate once I stopped trying to know it, eventually leading to everything that appeared to be revealing itself to be the kingdom of heaven. Then, there had been the awe and majesty that was the divine manifesting as the simplest things, like the bathroom sink, or terraced houses, eventually leading to the experience of everything that appeared to be as the divine manifesting in that form. And much later still there had arisen the presence, dispassionate awareness and joy that was always there whenever the sense of personal being was still and there was only living from a place of interiority.

Now I came to see that to some extent all these things had been forms of experience. They describe the various different forms of experience that had arisen for me, or 'here', as the whole process of the loss of apparent personal being deepened. But for this very reason, I now came to realise, they still involved some continuation of that very sense of personal being, because they were all the different ways in which things appeared to be *to* a subject of them - me. And with that I came to see that the very nature of all experience, including all so-called 'spiritual' experience, by definition, keeps something of the subject in place.

For that same reason what now arose became indescribable, because it was no longer an experience of a particular kind, the way things appeared to be to someone, the subject of them, but was simply what could be described as 'whatever was'. The problem is that even to describe in in these terms transforms what is being talked about through it becoming the object of analysis and description. Without an experiencer there is no such thing as 'whatever is or was'. That only arises when someone stops to look at it and tries to give words to it. Without an experiencer none of that is actually there at all.

Without a subject of experience, then, there is no experience. Therefore, there is no longer any sense of *how* things are, or *what* they are like – they just are. This simply cannot be put into words. It is infinitely close, because in the absence of an experiencing subject there is no apartness, and so no distance, but for this same reason it is also completely indescribable.

With this last shift, then, the sense of there being anyone apart who had any form of experience or to whom anything was really happening seemed to crumble away. And with that went the sense of there really being something, a person or entity, that was going anywhere at all, in the sense of a path leading from one place to another. This meant the end of the sense of being on any kind of journey, in this case a 'spiritual' journey, in which successive experiences seemed to be bringing about a gradual deepening of something, a gradual return to something. The result was an almost complete loss of interest in the journey itself. This was not something entirely new. The energy had gradually been emptying out of this journey, in the sense of it seeming like something interesting and worthwhile to talk about, for the previous year or two. This had seemed to happen to the same extent as the sense of 'personal' being had seemed to crumble away. The less of 'me' there was left the less interest this whole apparent process seemed to have. And now, with this more fundamental shift to a more constant impersonal reality, in which things still appear to happen but just not to me, the interest in the journey fizzled out completely. For a while I considered abandoning this book, seeing it as a description of something that no longer had any relevance or interest. But then, a while later, I came to see that though the experiences I have described are just that, experiences, and as such ephemeral and also grounded in some degree of 'personal' being, it was precisely through them that the very sense of 'personal' being had shattered and crumbled away. That is to say, through them an apparent ontological shift from 'personal' to impersonal/divine being had seemed to occur. Yes, it was only apparent and so not real and therefore it is true that nothing has really changed, but from a phenomenal perspective nothing could appear more fundamental than such a shift. What resulted was not just another form of experience, but another form of being.

Another way of trying to describe this is to say that with this latest shift removing the sense of there being any locus of experience, and that is to say an experiencer of these different forms of experience, they ceased to be forms of experience at all. So, there is no longer the living of interiority, there just is interiority; there is no longer an awareness of wholeness, there just is wholeness, there no longer is the living of the kingdom of heaven there just is the kingdom of heaven. Only none of this is anything that can ever really be described.

This has eventually transformed, though in a quite different as well as a deeper and more complete form, the living of unknowing which started so long ago after the weekend at Pax Lodge. This is no longer unknowing as a form of experience, but rather as the living of that which precedes all experience, all sense of a 'this' or a 'that'. It is the living of an unknown reality, as the simple mystery that everything is when no one is there to 'know' it. 'Knowing' here does not mean what is typically meant by knowledge in our society, knowing *that* 'this' or 'that'. That is propositional knowledge. This is the far wider, in fact ubiquitous, form of knowing that human beings are engaged in constantly in life and which gives rise to the whole nature of conceptualised experience, in which everything is subsumed under one concept or another and grasped *as* 'this' or 'that'. It is this that keeps the whole structure of subject and object in place, ultimately grounding the sense that 'I' am here and the 'world' is there. With the end of this form of knowing there is only a dwelling in an unknowing that is beyond the dichotomies of subject and object, 'me' and the 'world'. Both then disappear, subjective experience and the objective world, leaving only what is beyond words behind, the silent, wordless, indescribable mystery that is everything.

The irony and paradox of it all is so palpable. The more we try to know, the more we grasp at reality so as to possess it for ourselves in some way, the more we actually only reinforce the sense that we are here apart from everything and that only increases the sense that something is lost or missing that we need somehow to recover. This in turn gives rise to all the strategies by which we purportedly seek to let go of grasping and return to the simplicity of 'whatever is'. What we do not see, however, is that all those strategies are themselves simply another expression of the same grasping tendency and that they thereby keep the whole structure of self and separation in place. And so, the more we seek the more what we seek eludes us.

When stopping happens what is seen is that there never was any need to seek because everything that was ever sought *was* already. 'What is' is already whole, it is already complete. It is only because we grasp at it and try to possess it for ourselves in some way that it appears not to be. When that stops, when the sense of a 'person' or a separate subject falls or crumbles away, then we see that it was all only ever a wonderful irony and paradox. Because there never was the absence of anything, there never was any lack, there never was anything missing that needed to be found. Reality was always already perfectly whole just as it was. It only appeared not to be, it only ever appeared that there was something to find, because *we* were there looking for it.

*D I D 2 2 6 2 3 8 *

#0149 - 300718 - C0 - 210/148/11 - PB - DID2262338